For my wife, Heather

First published in Great Britain in 1999 by
Conran Octopus, a division of Octopus Publishing
Group Ltd

This edition published in 2007 by Bounty Books,
a division of Octopus Publishing Group Ltd
2–4 Heron Quays, London E14 4JP

An Hachette Livre UK Company

Managing Editor: Kate Bell

Editorial Assistant: Tanya Robinson

Copy Editor: Norma Macmillan

Editorial Consultant: Jenni Muir

Art Editor: Alison Fenton

Stylist: Wei Tang

Food for photography: Meg Jansz

Typesetting: Olivia Norton

Picture Research: Liz Boyd

Production: Julian Deeming

ISBN: 978-0-753716-37-3

A CIP catalogue record for this book is available from
the British Library

Printed and bound in China

Both metric and imperial measurements are given in this
book. Use either all metric or all imperial as the two are
not necessarily interchangeable.

Street Café
Brazil

Michael Bateman

Photography by Jeremy Hopley

 Bounty
Books

Contents

Introduction

Brazil is the land of exuberant Carnival and the insistent rhythm of the samba. Its colourful people love the pleasures of life, music, dance and food. Especially food. From the tropics of the Amazon north, which yield a cornucopia of exotic fruits, to the gaucho south where they rear meat, Brazilians enjoy a rich and varied cuisine. Nowhere is this more evident than in this huge country's street food. At any public event, food sellers materialize, peddling everything from freshly simmered corn-on-the-cob to coloured hard-boiled eggs.

Brazil has been a melting pot of food cultures from the sixteenth century onwards, a fusion of the food of the native Indians, the Portuguese colonizers and African slaves. Later, in the nineteenth century, other waves of immigrants added their contributions, first Italians and Spanish, then Poles and Lebanese and, more recently, Japanese. São Paulo, one of the world's biggest cities, with a population of 17 million, boasts the largest Japanese community outside Japan, and is home to literally thousands of *sushi* bars. And Italian pizza and pasta have become universal fare both in homes and in cafés.

Brazil is the largest country in Latin America, on a par with the United States in terms of size and population. The diversity of climate from north to south equates with the differences between the damp Loire Valley and the steaming rain forests and arid deserts of West and Central Africa. So in the south, you find cowboy types cooking steak on barbecues (the *churrascaria*), while in the north, the meat eaten is more likely to be *carne de sol* or *carne seco* (beef salted and dried in the sun). In the north, though, they enjoy a wealth of Amazon fish, wild game from the forest, vegetables such as chayote and jícama, and exotic fruits such as *graviola* (the succulent custard apple), *jabuticaba* (a cherry-sized acid fruit with a jellied texture), breadfruit, jackfruit and carambola or star fruit, not to mention papaya, mango, pineapple, guava and passion fruit.

Of all the fruit and vegetables that Brazil produces and exports none are more important than beans. Brazil is the world's largest grower and the biggest consumer. Black ones, brown ones, red and white ones. The small black beans *(feijão preto)* are the most prized. Beans and rice are eaten by most families every day, and the national dish (which Rio lays claim to) is *feijoada*, a rich, liquid stew of black beans in which half a dozen or more kinds of meat are submerged. *Feijoada* is colourfully served with white rice, butter-yellow *farofa* (the toasted flour milled from cassava), green stir-fried kale and rounds of sliced orange. It is traditionally preceded by a searingly strong rum sour called *caipirinha*, made with chopped limes crushed with sugar.

Brazilian food might have been a modest cuisine had it not been for the contribution made by the Africans, former slaves. Emancipated in the 1880s, they have made Bahia, their homeland in the north-east of Brazil, a by-word for imaginative cooking. What we see in Bahia is an early example of fusion cooking. The Portuguese came to Brazil, annexing the produce of the indigenous Indians – limes, avocados, sweetcorn, sweet potatoes, pumpkins, pineapples and peanuts. And for their part the Portuguese brought European foods, rice and sugar, olives and olive oil, coriander (the universal Brazilian herb) and, above all, the pig, and thus cured hams and sausages and lard for cooking.

The Africans in their turn introduced several kinds of palm from West Africa, one producing palm nut oil *(dendê)*, a thick, reddish, highly saturated oil that contributes perfume and flavour to any dish cooked with it. Another palm, the coconut palm, provides its multi-purpose nuts which contain a liquid *(água de coco)* that is such a refreshing and cooling drink on a hot day. The white grated flesh and the milk made from it feature in both savoury and sweet dishes. And, since the hot north-east is alien to the growing of wheat, the Africans, needing a starchy base for subsistence, brought over cassava, a hairy, white-fleshed root as thick as a mug. The flour when toasted is called *farofa*, and is sprinkled like a condiment on many dishes.

So it was that, when these several food cultures and all these disparate ingredients met, there was a gastronomic 'big bang' and *Cozinha Baiana* (Bahaian cuisine) was the result. The most popular dishes are based on seafood and shellfish – fish soups (with coconut milk, lime juice, coriander and chillies), simple fish stews *(moqueca)* with sliced onion, tomatoes and green peppers, dyed yellow with *dendê* oil, and the local speciality, baked stuffed crab, *recheadas de siri*.

Hot chillies are in evidence here, usually incorporated in the food, while in other parts of Brazil freshly made hot chilli sauces or *salsas* are always served at the table. They are mostly made from the *malagueta* chilli, a witheringly hot, very small variety native to Brazil.

Sweet dishes are adored in Brazil and served at every meal. A breakfast spread in Le Meridien hotel in Copacabana offers not only a dozen ripe tropical fruits, but rich caramel *pudim*, coconut flan *(quindão)*, cooling *manjar blanco* (a delicious wedge of blancmange made with coconut milk), succulent breads made with cornmeal, banana and coconut, and unusual preserves called *cocadas* – caramelized beetroot, carrot, pineapple, mixtures of pumpkin and coconut, guava paste, quince paste.

The recipes chosen for this book only begin to touch on a wide-ranging, vibrant and exciting cuisine that is Brazil's. Read, taste, enjoy.

The Brazilian storecupboard

Abóbora *The Brazilian orange-fleshed pumpkin has a dense, firm flesh, similar to butternut and kabocha squashes. It can be eaten on its own, added to soups and purées, or made into pie fillings and desserts.*

Avocado (abacate) *Brazil has many varieties of avocado, from smooth to rough-skinned, small to very large. Avocados are enjoyed in savoury salads, but also, unusually, as a dessert, the flesh creamed with sugar and then chilled.*

Banana *In the markets you see bananas of every shade of colour and every size. Some are actually plantains, only used in cooking. These are usually cut into chip-sized pieces and fried.*

Beans (feijão) *Feijão preto (black beans) are the most prized, being used in the national dish. They are small and as shiny as black pearls when first washed, and cook to a thick, coal-black purée. They are sometimes sold as turtle beans. The more common bean is a beige-brown bean called* mulatinho. *The black-eyed bean (fradinho) is used to make* acarajé, *crispy fritters flavoured with ground dried prawns.*

Cachaça *A white rum, also known as* aguardente, *made from sugar cane. Numerous varieties exist, of every quality, from fire water to premium brands. In Rio de Janeiro, a restaurant called the Academia da Cachaça stocks 2,000 varieties, the oldest from 1875.*

Cassava (mandioca or macaxeira) *Also called manioc root and yuca, this starchy root contains poisonous toxins and must be processed to remove these before drying and grinding. The flour (farinha de mandioca) is coarse, like maize flours (you can find it, labelled as gari, in West Indian and Asian shops). When toasted in a dry pan it becomes known as farofa and as such it is sprinkled on many foods in the north-east, rather like a condiment. When fried in dendê or butter to make it yellow it is called farofa amarela. Another variety of cassava, aipim, contains little poison, mostly in the skin, and is edible after cooking. Aipim is sold in markets to be used just like potatoes, boiled or fried. Tapioca is derived from cassava.*

Chayote (xuxu) *This green, apple-sized vegetable, also known as christophine, is much liked in Brazil. When boiled it has the character of cooked cucumber and it is often baked in a cheese sauce, like marrow. It also works well in chilled salads with onions and fruit, providing a crunchy texture.*

Chilli (pimenta) *Pimenta-do-cheiro ('cheiro' means aroma) is a tiny round red or yellow chilli, half the size of an olive. Pimentas-do-cheiro are normally bottled in a mild vinegar. Pimenta malagueta, Brazil's seriously hot chilli, is similar to Caribbean or Scotch bonnet peppers. Both red (very hot) and green (not quite so hot) are served at the table either bottled or in freshly made sauces, with most meals. Malaguetas are also bottled in vinegar, in oil or in cachaça, or blended with liquid from a stew or soup. Brazilian cooks use little hot spicing in the preparation of a dish, leaving the amount of chilli heat to be added by individual diners to taste.*

Chorizo (chouriço) *The blanket name for all kinds of cured sausage, sometimes mild, sometimes piquant, sometimes smoked. It is usually used in cooking, fried then added to bean stews. Lingüiça is a long sausage, usually sold doubled into a u-shape.*

Coconut (côco) *Green, or unripe, coconuts are sold by the roadside, split in front of you with a machete and served as a refreshing drink. The flesh can be scraped away like creamy paste. Once mature, the coconut, now brown and hairy, is used in cooking. The liquid inside, água de côco, is lovely for drinking, and the white flesh, grated, is a key ingredient in desserts, pastries and cakes as well as being used to make coconut milk, essential in many seafood stews and countless other savoury dishes.*

Coriander (coentro) *This is the most popular Brazilian herb, used freely as an ingredient and a garnish.*

Dried prawn (camarão seco) *An essential but pungent ingredient in Bahia, this is used like a condiment to impart a salty, seafood flavour. Fishermen moisten the prawns with* dendê *oil before laying them to dry, and half fry, in the burning sun for several days, raking them over from time to time. Large ones are often sold smoked.*

Dried salt cod (bacalhau) *Imported from northern waters,* bacalhau *is part of the colonial Portuguese tradition. It must be soaked overnight in several changes of water to remove the salt, but then it needs only brief cooking, after which it must be carefully boned and skinned. The flesh is mixed with onion and tomato in savoury purées and stews, or with a starchy base such as potatoes to make croquettes and* bolinhos, *little deep-fried balls.*

Graviola *Also called* fruta do conde, pinha *or* ata, *this is similar to the custard apple or cherimoya. It looks like a large, green-skinned, closed pine cone. The custardy flesh, tasting of pears and melons, is used in desserts after the shiny black pips have been removed.*

Guava (goiaba) *The guava is loved for its perfume and tart flavour. It is used in drinks and sorbets, and to make a paste called* goiabada, *eaten at breakfast with white cheese.*

Kale (couve) *The most important hearty green vegetable in Brazil, kale is always eaten with a Saturday* feijoada, *finely shredded and stir-fried.*

Lime (limão) *Brazil has no lemons, and* limão *is often mistranslated as lemon; however, its vivid green colour and powerful fragrance soon make it clear that the* limão *is a (superior) world away from other citrus fruits. It is essential in most Brazilian dishes, not least in the cocktail* caipirinha.

Mango (manga) *Originally brought from India, the mango has truly acclimatized itself to northern Brazil, where the abundant fruit crashes down from huge trees the height of oaks.*

Okra (quiabo) *In Bahia, okra is also known as* cararu — *the name given to an okra and dried prawn purée.*

Palm hearts (palmito) *Harvested and canned, these are the size of the white of large leeks, and not unsimilar in their silky texture. An obligatory hors-d'oeuvre or salad ingredient in Latin America, palm hearts harmonize well with delicate seasonings and dressings.*

Palm nut oil (dendê) *Deep yellow or reddish, thick and strong-flavoured, this is the cooking medium of the north-east.*

It is not one of the world's most healthy vegetable oils, being as highly saturated as animal fat.

Papaya *Also known as paw paw, these have an umistakable rich perfume when ripe. Larger varieties are known as* mamão *and have lurid orange flesh. Best served with a squeeze of lime juice.*

Passion fruit (maracujá) *This is probably Brazil's favourite flavour in drinks. The yellow, red and purple* maracujá *seen in markets are much bigger than those sold in Europe, more tart in flavour and slightly less perfumed.*

Pineapple (abacaxi) *Native to Brazil, fresh pineapple juice makes sublime alcoholic drinks such as* batida, *mixed with the white rum,* cachaça.

Sun-dried salted beef (carne de sol) *This is bought in salty chunks and needs to be soaked overnight in several changes of water to get rid of saltiness before it is used for stews.*

Ingredients illustrated on previous pages
Top row (*left to right*) *cassava flour and cassava root; black beans and black-eyed beans; dried salt cod and dried prawns; limes; pineapple; kale and coriander.*
Middle row (*left to right*) *graviola; dendê oil; chorizo and* lingüiça; *tapioca flour and tapioca pearls;* pimenta-do-cheiro *and* pimenta malagueta; *coconut and palm hearts.*
Bottom row (*left to right*) *mango and passion fruit; papaya; chayotes; bananas and plantains; white rum* (cachaça); *guavas.*

The Brazilian kitchen

Cooking the Brazilian way requires no mystifying pieces of equipment, neither strange-shaped pots or pans nor bamboo basket steamers, neither special knives nor chopsticks.

In Brazil's southern states the outdoor cook will be at home, because much of the meat is cooked on a barbecue, or *churrascaria*, a technique that requires no more than a pair of tongs and, in the case of the Brazilians, a mug of salted water to splash on the meat (this prevents the meat from producing a hard, resistant crust, so it cooks through better).

In the big cities, such as São Paulo and Rio de Janeiro, cooking-ware is straightforward: large saucepans for cooking beans, smaller saucepans with tight-fitting lids for rice and deep ceramic casseroles into which beans and meat are sometimes decanted to finish cooking in the oven. Hefty wooden spoons and potato ricers are essential too, to mash cooked beans for soups and sauces, plus various forms of sieve to make them into purées.

Most homes will have a pressure cooker for beans, which reduces the cooking time from 3 hours or so to about 30 minutes. There will be at least a once-a-week bean cook-up. The first beans will be eaten as they are. The next day they are usually heated up, fried in oil or lard, and mashed (*refritos* – literally refried). Subsequent servings see them return in the form of purées and soups.

The oven is much used, both for the baking of savoury pastries and for the numerous sweets, custards, flans and fruit breads. But the wide range of dishes, moulds and cake, bread and patty tins is no different from those used anywhere else. The frying pan is essential, too. Chicken croquettes, prawns with their shells on, *picadinhos* (little pieces of meat) and pork crackling *(torresmos)* are all cooked to a crisp in the frying pan. A *frigideira* is an iron oven-proof frying pan which can be used both on top of the stove and in the oven.

Many of the *salgadinhos* (bite-sized snacks) emerge from the deep-fryer, such as the *bolinhos* (deep-fried balls of shrimp, ham, salt cod and rice). The deep-fryer is even more essential in the north-east where the unique cooking of Bahia derives much of its character and flavour from the use of the thick, orange-coloured palm nut cooking oil, *dendê*. Street sellers set up a deep pan of simmering oil on the pavement and deep-fry the little bean fritters, *acarajé*, to order.

In some regions you find specialized pots. In Minas Gerais, for example, they use black stoneware casseroles for a *tutú à mineira* (their version of a *feijoada*, in which the beans are mashed to a purée). In the Amazon north, off the island of Marajoara, they use two-handled tall terracotta vessels that resemble Roman amphorae.

A tough grater, or the grater attachment on a food processor, is a vital kitchen utensil, given the importance of grated coconut in Brazilian cuisine. Screwdrivers and hammers are best suited to dealing with the shell. Roasting split coconuts for 30 minutes in a hot oven develops the flavour and makes them easier to grate.

Food processors and blenders have taken the place of the pestle and mortar for many basic Brazilian kitchen techniques, especially in the north-east — making mushy purées, pounding soaked black-eyed beans for *acarajé* and pounding dried prawns. But the mortar still has its place in every kitchen, and is always used to mash avocados or to break up chopped limes for a *caipirinha*.

Tropical fruit is an essential part of the Brazilian table so a juicer has to be a good investment. The health-conscious Brazilian consumes vast quantities of fruit and vegetable juices, either on their own (a *suco*), as a milk shake (a *vitamina*) or mixed with alcohol (*batida*).

Making coconut milk

Coconut milk – the creamy liquid extracted from the grated flesh – is one of the most important ingredients in Brazilian cooking. If you cannot get fresh coconuts it is easy to make with desiccated coconut. Or use one of the prepared coconut products on the market, the best being coconut milk in cans. Coconut milk powder and compressed blocks are also available.

To make coconut milk using a fresh coconut, first pierce holes in two of the three indented 'eyes' at the base of the nut using a hammer and large nail or tough screwdriver. Pour out the liquid into a container, straining it through a sieve or muslin to remove any dust or debris from the shell. To open the shell, find a good hard surface and, using a hammer, tap the shell firmly and repeatedly across the middle until it breaks apart. Use a heavy blunt knife to separate shards of flesh from the shell, then cut off the hard brown skin from the pieces of flesh.

It can be painful work to grate coconut flesh using a household grater, so it's preferable to use the grater on an electric food mixer or food processor. An average coconut will yield about 175–225 g/6–8 oz grated coconut flesh. Put the grated coconut in a bowl and pour on 125 ml/4 fl oz hot but not boiling water. Leave to soak for 10 minutes. Then line a sieve with muslin or a cotton cloth and pour the soaked coconut into it. Gather up the ends, fold them over and squeeze out the liquid as if you were wringing out a T-shirt. Set this liquid aside.

Repeat the process, using 500 ml/18 fl oz hot water. This will produce a thinner but still tasty liquid. Mix together the first and second pressings and you have 625 ml/just over 1 pint coconut milk. If you leave it to stand, a layer of thick 'cream' will rise to the surface, and this can be skimmed off and used for a richer result. (Canned coconut milk will also separate in this way, so the can should be shaken before opening, unless you want the richer cream from the top.)

To make coconut milk with desiccated coconut, use 125 g/4 oz coconut with 250 ml/9 fl oz hot water for the first pressing and 375 ml/12 fl oz water for the second pressing; this will yield 500 ml/18 fl oz coconut milk. Or use powdered instant coconut, allowing 75 g/3 oz to 500 ml/18 fl oz water to make the same volume.

Below *Prawn Pastries (page 28)*

SOUPS
AND STARTERS

Stuffed Eggs

Ovos Recheados

Some dishes that originated in Europe — where they have all but died out — live on in Latin America, and none more so than stuffed eggs. They appear in many guises among the varied appetizers that are offered on celebratory occasions. In Bahia, ovos reacheados may be served with Coconut and Prawn Cream (page 79) and a dusting of Golden Cassava Flour (page 72). Ovos recheados can be filled with many appetizing stuffings, such as shredded tuna in mayonnaise spiced with malagueta chilli, garnished with halved green or black olives or a sprinkling of chopped parsley or fresh coriander. **Makes 16**

8 free-range eggs

2 tablespoons grated white breadcrumbs

50 g/1¾ oz Parmesan or other hard cheese *freshly grated*

30 g/1 oz butter *melted*

sea salt and freshly ground black pepper

1 Preheat the oven to 200°C/400°F/gas 6.

2 Hard-boil the eggs for 4–6 minutes. Peel under cold running water. When cool, cut in half lengthways. Set the whites aside and put the yolks in a bowl.

3 Pound the egg yolks, mixing in the breadcrumbs, cheese, butter and a seasoning of salt and pepper. Using a teaspoon, form the mixture into neat shapes similar to egg yolks, and stuff the egg white halves.

4 Place in an oven dish, cover with foil and heat through in the oven for 10 minutes.

Chicken Soup

Canja

Every country has its nourishing chicken soup, which is intended to bring comfort and solace. Brazil is no exception. **Serves 6–8**

1 Place the chicken in a large saucepan and cover with 2 litres/3½ pints water. Add the onions, 2 of the carrots, the tomatoes, celery, coriander or parsley, celery leaves, peppercorns and salt.

2 Bring to the boil, skimming off the scum that comes to surface. Turn down the heat and simmer for 2 hours.

3 Remove the chicken from the broth and, when cool enough to handle, remove and discard the skin. Pull the meat from the bones and cut into strips. Strain the broth, discarding the vegetables which will have passed on their goodness to the broth. Return the chicken meat to the saucepan together with the rice and the remaining carrots.

4 Bring back to the boil and simmer for a further 30 minutes. Season to taste before serving.

1 boiling fowl

500 g/1 lb 2 oz onions *quartered*

4 carrots *sliced*

500 g/1 lb 2 oz tomatoes or 1 x 400 g/14 oz can whole tomatoes *drained and seeded*

2 sticks celery *sliced*

small bunch of fresh coriander or parsley *chopped*

3–4 celery leaves

12 black peppercorns

1 teaspoon sea salt

100 g/3½ oz long-grain white rice

Pumpkin Soup

Quibebe

Although abóbora, *the squash used for this soup, translates as 'pumpkin', it is not the watery giant Hallowe'en vegetable. The Brazilian pumpkin is a dense-textured member of the American squash family. The close texture and rich, sweet taste of this squash make it attractive for both sweet fillings in desserts and savoury soups such as this, beloved of the African community of Bahia.* **Serves 6**

1 Halve the *abóbora*, remove the seeds and fibres with a large spoon and pare away the hard peel. Cut the flesh into bite-sized chunks, about 2.5 cm/1 in square.

2 Heat the oil in a frying pan and cook the onion until it softens and starts to turn yellow. Add the garlic and cook for 1 more minute. Stir in the chilli to heat through. Finally, add the tomato and tomato purée. Heat, stirring, to blend the flavours thoroughly, then transfer to a saucepan.

3 Add the *abóbora* pieces and the stock to the saucepan and bring to the boil. Turn down the heat to low, cover with a lid and simmer for 20–30 minutes or until the *abóbora* breaks up into a purée. Whisk it with a fork or put in a blender or food processor briefly. Add salt to taste and stir well.

4 Serve with chilli sauce and grated cheese, to be added as you like.

1 kg/2¼ lb *abóbora* **(or use butternut or kabocha squash)**

4 tablespoons *dendê* **oil (or use olive oil or butter)**

1 onion *finely chopped*

1 garlic clove *crushed then chopped*

1 fresh red chilli *sliced into fine rounds* **(optional)**

1 large tomato *skinned, seeded and chopped*

2 teaspoons tomato purée

850 ml/1½ pints chicken or beef stock

sea salt

To serve:

Tabasco or West Indian chilli sauce

grated Cheddar or Parmesan cheese

Golden Chicken Savouries

Coxinhas de Galinha

Appetizers (salgadinhos) *which have been egg-and-breadcrumbed and then deep-fried have a long European tradition. The Brazilians are masters of this preparation too. Every sort of mixture — based on potatoes, cassava, vegetables, fish, beef, pork or chicken — can be assembled to make croquettes, rissoles and such like.* Coxinhas *are bound with a pastry skin, so they don't fall apart in cooking.* **Makes about 12**

corn oil

1.5 kg/3 lb 5 oz chicken
cut into 8 joints

½ onion *finely chopped*

1 garlic clove *crushed then chopped*

**sea salt and freshly ground
black pepper**

white breadcrumbs for coating

For the dough:

250 g/9 oz rice flour

500 ml/18 fl oz milk

100 g/3½ oz butter *softened*

3 free-range egg yolks

few drops of chilli sauce

To serve:

Chilli Salsa (see page 21)

1 Heat a little oil in a heavy-bottomed flameproof casserole or saucepan and brown the chicken joints on both sides. Add enough water to cover the bottom of the pan, then cover and cook gently until the chicken is tender, 20–30 minutes. Drain, reserving the cooking juices for the dough.

2 When the chicken is cool enough to handle, pick the meat away from bones and skin (they can be used in stock). Cut the breasts into 12 long strips – they will be the core of each *coxinha*. Chop or mince the remainder of the meat finely and mix with the chopped onion, garlic, salt and pepper.

3 In another bowl, mix the rice flour with the milk and enough of the reserved chicken cooking juices to make a stiff dough. Mix in the butter and the egg yolks to make a soft dough. Stir in the minced chicken. Season to taste, adding a little chilli sauce.

4 Divide the dough into 12 equal lumps. Take a piece of chicken breast and roll a piece of dough round it, forming into the shape of chicken leg. (Some cooks reserve pieces of chicken bone and push a knobbly end into each shaped piece to simulate the leg bone and serve as a useful handle.)

5 Roll the shaped pieces in breadcrumbs. Deep-fry in hot corn oil at 180°C/350°F, in batches, until golden brown all over. Drain on kitchen paper and serve hot with the Chilli Salsa.

Cheese Croquettes
Croquettes de Queijo

Among the most common snacks in Brazil, these are served at any time of the day, from breakfast to supper. Smaller versions can be served as part of a mixed presentation of salgadinhos. **Makes about 12**

1 Preheat the oven to 180°C/350°F/gas 4.

2 In a bowl, rub the butter into the flour, then mix in the egg yolk followed by the breadcrumbs, cheese and a seasoning of salt and pepper. If the mixture is too dry add a spoonful of water to help bind it together. Shape the mixture into balls slightly smaller than the size of an egg.

3 Oil or butter a baking tray. Whisk the egg white lightly in a bowl, dip each croquette into it and place on the tray. Bake for 25–30 minutes or until brown and crisp, checking if the croquettes are cooked after 20 minutes. Serve hot with Chilli Salsa.

55 g/2 oz butter *diced*

150 g/5 oz plain flour

1 free-range egg *separated*

55 g/2 oz dry white breadcrumbs *finely grated*

55 g/2 oz Parmesan or other hard cheese *freshly grated*

sea salt and freshly ground black pepper

Chilli Salsa

*A small saucer of this salsa (*molho de campanha*) accompanies almost every main dish in Brazil, be it meat grills, stews, fish, beans or rice. In a bowl, mix together 1 red onion (or any mild onion) chopped into small pieces, 1 large tomato skinned, seeded and diced, 2 tablespoons red wine vinegar, 1 garlic clove crushed then chopped, 2 tablespoons olive oil or sunflower oil (optional), 1 tablespoon chopped fresh coriander or flat-leaf parsley, a few drops of* malagueta *chilli oil or other chilli sauce and salt and pepper to taste. Taste and adjust the seasonings to get a good balance of hot, salt, sour and smooth. Chill for 1 hour or so, to allow the flavours to blend. For molho apimentada, add a ladle of liquid from cooked beans, or a stew. For molho de limão, use the juice of 2 limes instead of red wine vinegar.*

Sweetcorn Parcels

Pamonha de Milho Verde

The most common street food in São Paulo, this is a tasty sweetcorn mixture wrapped in its own husks and steamed. Unsweetened, with a little salt added instead of sugar, these are also served at parties with other appetizers, and may be eaten warm or cold. They must be made with fresh, not canned, sweetcorn. **Makes 16**

8 young corn on the cob in their husks

125 ml/4 fl oz milk

caster sugar to taste

15 g/½ oz butter *softened*

1 Remove the sweetcorn from their husks, reserving all the green leaves but discarding the silk. Separate the best 8 inner leaves.

2 With a grater, shred the sweetcorn kernels off the cobs into a bowl. Drain the grated sweetcorn, then put it into a blender. Add the milk and blend until quite smooth and thick. Sweeten to taste, and beat in the butter.

3 Divide the mixture into 8 equal portions using a tablespoon. Shape each portion into a ball and wrap in one of the inner leaves. Fold the two long edges inwards, to enclose the mixture, then wrap the ends over to make a tight parcel. Tie with kitchen string or fasten with elastic bands.

4 Line the top half of a steamer with the outer leaves of the corn husks and place the parcels on top, seam side up. Steam for about 50 minutes, or until the husks have turned yellow. Make sure the water doesn't boil dry beneath them.

5 The stuffing will be quite sticky, so you need to leave the parcels to cool for 15 minutes before serving.

Little Cheese Custards

Queijadinhas

Mixtures of sweet and savoury are typical of Brazil. These little mouthfuls of a sweet-savoury custard are baked in tiny waxed paper cases such as are used for petit-fours. They will keep for a few days in an airtight tin or in a plastic container in the fridge.
Serves 6 (makes about 24)

1 x 450 g/15 oz can condensed milk

2 free-range egg yolks

70 g/2½ oz freshly grated coconut (or use desiccated coconut)

2 teaspoons freshly grated Parmesan cheese

1 Preheat the oven to 200°C/400°F/gas 6.

2 In a bowl beat together the condensed milk, egg yolks, coconut and Parmesan with a wooden spoon.

3 Fill 24 waxed paper sweet cases with the mixture. Lay a sheet of aluminium foil in a wide oven tin and set the cases on the foil. Fold up the sides of the foil all round and pinch at the corners to make a waterproof boat for the paper cases.

4 Place the tin on the oven shelf and pour boiling water from a kettle into the tin, to half fill the space round the foil boat. Bake for 30 minutes. Leave to cool before serving.

Little Balls of Rice

Bolinhos de Arroz

This snack or appetizer is similar to one in Italy (arancini di riso) *which uses cooked risotto rice, but this is lighter.* **Makes about 10**

1 Mix together all the ingredients in a bowl with a wooden spoon. On a floured board, shape into walnut-sized balls by pressing each one into a tablespoon, sprinkling with more flour as necessary.

2 Heat oil for deep-frying to 180°C/350°F, then fry the rice balls, a few at a time, until golden all over. Drain on kitchen paper and serve hot.

250 g/9 oz cooked long-grain white rice *cold*

1 free-range egg *beaten*

2 heaped tablespoons plain flour

1 tablespoon milk

2 spring onions *finely chopped*

sprig of parsley or fresh coriander *finely chopped*

sea salt and freshly ground black pepper

oil for deep-frying

Chorizo Rolls

Enroladinhos

These are attractive salgadinhos *(appetizers), designed to be eaten in one bite with drinks. Ask your deli for a mild chorizo — or* chouriçou *in a Portuguese shop — as there are many varieties.* **Makes about 40**

1 Wrap the bread in a damp tea cloth and leave for 1 hour to ensure that the bread is elastic and pliable for rolling.

2 Remove the crusts from the bread slices.

3 Beat the egg yolks in a shallow dish with 1 teaspoon water and a seasoning of salt, pepper and cayenne.

4 Dip each slice of bread in beaten egg to moisten, then roll it round a length of chorizo, pegging it in place with halved wooden cocktail sticks.

5 Cover the bottom of a frying pan with a film of oil and, when really hot, fry the rolls until golden all over. Remove and cut each one across into 1 cm/½ in lengths. Serve as part of mixed appetizers.

10 slices white bread

3 free-range egg yolks

sea salt and freshly ground black pepper

cayenne pepper

200 g/7 oz chorizo

oil for frying

Prawn Pastries
Empadinhas de Camarão

Empadinhas (or empadas) are the quintessential street food of Brazil, with various stuffings — spicy minced chicken, ham, cheese, vegetables, potato and, especially, prawn. Made with short pastry, they are both appetizing and filling. **Makes 12–20**

For the pastry:

500 g/1 lb 2 oz plain flour

½ teaspoon salt

250 g/9 oz butter or lard *softened but not melted*

2 free-range egg yolks

For the marinade:

juice of 1 lime

1 garlic clove *crushed then chopped*

sea salt and freshly ground black pepper

For the filling:

175 g/6 oz peeled prawns, preferably raw *chopped if large*

olive oil for frying

350 g/12 oz onions *finely chopped*

1 green pepper *seeded and chopped*

250 g/9 oz tomatoes *skinned and seeded* **or 1 x 400 g/14 oz can whole tomatoes** *drained and seeded*

1 teaspoon tomato purée

sprig of fresh coriander *finely chopped*

1 teaspoon cornflour

12 black olives *stoned and chopped*

1 To make the pastry, sift the flour and salt into a bowl and rub in the fat with your fingertips until the mixture is crumb-like. Add one of the egg yolks and about 3 tablespoons water to bind to a stiff but kneadable dough. Roll into a ball, cover with cling film and chill for 1 hour.

2 Meanwhile, put the prawns in a bowl with the lime juice, garlic and some salt and pepper and leave to marinate for 30 minutes.

3 Heat a little olive oil in a frying pan and cook the chopped onions and green pepper until softened. Add the tomatoes, tomato purée and coriander and cook for a few more minutes to blend the flavours. Add the prawns and their marinade to the frying pan and pour in enough water (up to half a wineglass) to moisten. Simmer for 10 minutes. Mix the cornflour with 2 teaspoons cold water, add to the prawn mixture and stir until thickened. Add the olives, check the seasoning and leave to cool.

4 Preheat the oven to 200°C/400°F/gas 6. Meanwhile, roll out the pastry on a floured board to about 3 mm/⅛ in thickness. Using a 4–5 cm/1½–2 in pastry cutter, or the rim of a suitable glass, cut out 24–40 rounds. Place a dessertspoonful of the prawn mixture on half of the pastry rounds, without overfilling them. Using a pastry brush, moisten the edges with water, then set another pastry round on top of each and pinch the edges with your thumb to seal. Beat the remaining egg yolk and brush over each pastry to glaze. Arrange on baking trays and bake for about 20 minutes, or until golden brown. Serve hot.

Golden Fried Squid

Lula Frita

Squid can be disappointing if not cooked properly, for it very quickly toughens. It must be cooked for either a long time – up to 3 hours in a stew – to tenderize it, or, conversely, in less than a minute and served before it hardens up. Quick-fried squid can be served as bite-sized appetizers skewered on cocktail sticks. **Serves 4**

1 Clean the squid under running water, rubbing away any dark skin. Separate the tentacles, which can also be cooked. Slit open the pocket of the body and scrape away the inside with the back of a knife; discard. Rinse well. Cut the squid into 2.5–4 cm/1–1½ in squares. Mop dry on kitchen paper.

2 Shake some flour into a soup bowl and add a seasoning of salt, pepper and cayenne.

3 Heat a thin layer of oil in a wide pan until very hot. Dip the squares of squid and the tentacles in the seasoned flour and fry quickly until golden brown on both sides. (Cook them in batches rather than fill the pan, which would bring down the temperature of the cooking oil.)

4 Drain on kitchen paper, squeeze lime juice on top and serve with an optional dipping sauce of Chilli Salsa.

1 kg/2¼ lb fresh squid

plain flour for dredging

sea salt and freshly ground black pepper

cayenne pepper

oil for frying

juice of 1 lime

To serve:

Chilli Salsa (see page 21) (optional)

Bean Cakes

Acarajé

These are the most renowned street snacks of northern Brazil, particularly in Bahia where they are sold at the pavement edge by women in colourful costumes. Acarajé fritters have their origin in mainland Africa, but what makes these black-eyed bean cakes unique to Brazil is the addition of prawn paste and chilli to give an extra dimension of flavour and piquancy. If you find the smell of dried prawns too pungent you can omit them. The bean cakes will still be delicious. **Makes about 20**

450 g/1 lb dried black-eyed beans *slightly crushed in a food processor to split the skins, then soaked for at least 4 hours or overnight*

55 g/2 oz dried prawns

olive oil for frying

1 medium onion *coarsely chopped*

¼ teaspoon cayenne pepper or chilli powder

sea salt

***dendê* oil for deep-frying (or use corn oil)**

To serve:

Chilli Salsa (see page 21) (optional)

Coconut and Prawn Cream (see page 79) (optional)

1 Drain the black-eyed beans, then put them in a bowl of water and rub them vigorously between your hands to remove the skins. Use several changes of water. The skins will rise to the surface and can be skimmed off and discarded. Finally, cover with very hot, but not boiling, water and leave to soak until cool enough for you to rub off any remaining skins.

2 Put the dried prawns in a pan and cover with water. Bring to the boil then simmer for 1 minute. Drain then rinse in cold water. Dry the prawns on kitchen paper then fry in a little olive oil for 1–2 minutes or until crisp. Chop roughly. In a blender or food processor, in small batches, purée the black-eyed beans, prawns and onion to make a thick paste. Season with the cayenne or chilli powder and salt (carefully, as the prawns may be salty). Heat a 7.5 cm/3 in layer of oil in a deep pan to 180°C/350°F.

3 Using a dessertspoon, scoop up the paste and press into neat, compact oval shapes, smoothing them with your fingers. Deep-fry, in small batches of 5 or 6 at a time, for about 4 minutes, or until golden. After each batch, bring the temperature of the oil back to 180°C/350°F and use a slotted spoon to skim off any detached crumbs of bean cake which will otherwise burn. Drain the fried cakes on kitchen paper, and keep warm.

4 Serve whole or split open with Chilli Salsa or Coconut and Prawn Cream.

Married Prawns

Camarãos Casadinhos

One of the most attractive finger foods, this consists of two prawns stuffed with cassava flour and skewered together, head to tail, with a wooden cocktail stick. **Serves 4**

16 large raw prawns in shell, with heads

juice of 4–6 limes

1 garlic clove *crushed then chopped*

2 teaspoons chopped fresh coriander

sea salt and freshly ground black pepper

30 g/1 oz cassava flour

knob of butter

sunflower oil for frying

To serve:

lime quarters

1 Remove the 'whiskers' from the prawns, but do not peel them or remove the heads. Mix together the lime juice, garlic, coriander and salt and pepper to taste in a bowl. Add the prawns and toss to coat, then leave to marinate for 1 hour in a cool place. Drain and mop dry with kitchen paper.

2 Prepare the stuffing by heating the cassava flour in a frying pan, stirring in the butter and cooking until the flour takes on a golden colour (see Golden Cassava Flour, page 72). Remove from the heat.

3 With a sharp knife make a deep incision lengthways in each prawn, to cut open the underside. Stuff with the cassava flour mixture. Using wooden cocktail sticks, skewer pairs of prawns together, head to tail.

4 Fry in a shallow film of very hot oil for about 2 minutes on each side or until crispy and pink. Serve hot, garnished with quartered limes.

Spicy Stuffed Corn Husks

Abará

This is an ideal finger food, a neat envelope of corn husk (or folded banana leaf) enclosing a spicy filling. The filling is almost identical to Bean Cakes (page 30), though here it is steamed and not deep-fried. A similar dish, called acaçá, *where the filling is a paste of unseasoned white cornmeal mixed with ground prawns, is eaten in honour of the deity Oxalá, known in Bahia as Candomblé, who is associated with voodoo rituals. Although not authentic, greaseproof paper or even foil can be used to make the envelopes for steaming and the filling then transferred to lettuce leaves for serving.* **Serves 6 (makes 12)**

1 Soak the black-eyed beans in water overnight, or for at least 5 hours. Drain, then put into a bowl of fresh water. Rub the beans between your fingers to loosen the skins, which will float to the surface and can then be skimmed off. If the skins are resistant, pour boiling water over the beans and leave for 10 minutes before skinning. Drain the beans again.

2 Grind the beans in a blender, in batches, adding some of the oil to make them easier to blend. Transfer to a bowl.

3 Stirring with a wooden spoon, mix in the ground prawns, onion, ginger and salt to taste. Divide into 12 equal portions.

4 Plunge the corn husks or banana leaves into boiling water to soften them, then drain and pat dry. Roll a portion of the bean mixture between your palms to make an oblong and wrap tightly in a corn husk or leaf. Tie closed with raffia or cord (or use an elastic band). Make the remaining envelopes in the same way.

5 Place in a steamer, cover and steam for 20 minutes. Cut the raffia or cord before serving.

800 g/1¾ lb dried black-eyed beans

125 ml/4 fl oz *dendê* oil (or use olive oil)

55 g/2 oz dried prawns *ground in a mortar or food processor*

1 onion *very finely chopped*

2.5 cm/1 in piece fresh ginger *peeled and grated*

sea salt

For the wrapping (optional):

fresh green corn husks or 12 pieces banana leaf *each about 15 cm/6 in square*

Lime Marinated Fish

Ceviche

Ceviche *may well have developed from* escabeche *(page 36), in which poached or fried fish is marinated in an acidulated mixture.* Ceviche *uses the sour juice of limes or lemons to 'cook' thin fillets of raw fish. Recipes for* ceviche *are found all along the coast of Brazil and throughout Latin America. It is especially good when the fish is spanking fresh.*

Serves 4

1 Cut the fillets into flat strips about 2.5 cm/1 in long.

2 To make the marinade, slit open the red chillies lengthways and scrape out seeds and membranes. Chop into fine crescents. In a shallow dish, combine the chillies, lime or lemon juice, onion, garlic, coriander and a seasoning of salt and pepper. Toss the fish strips in this mixture, then leave to marinate in the refrigerator for at least 30 minutes, or until the fish turns opaque. Do not marinate for longer than 2 hours.

3 Drain the fish, discarding the marinade, and mix with the diced tomato. Serve with a decorative garnish of quartered limes, coriander leaves, whole red and green chillies and chopped spring onion.

450 g/1 lb fillets of fresh sea bass or other fine-quality fish

1 large tomato *skinned, seeded and diced*

For the marinade:

2 fresh red chillies

juice of 4 limes or lemons, or some of each

1 mild red onion or the white parts of 1 bunch of spring onions *thinly sliced*

1 garlic clove *crushed then chopped*

2 sprigs of fresh coriander *chopped*

sea salt and freshly ground black pepper

To serve:

lime quarters

1 sprig of fresh coriander *leaves kept whole*

4 fresh chillies (2 green and 2 red)

2 spring onions *both white and green roughly chopped*

Soused Fish

Escabeche

The Portuguese and Spanish brought escabeche *to Latin America. This dish of fried fish pickled in a cooked vinegar marinade is not only tasty, it is an effective form of preservation in hot countries. It was developed by the Arabs who used the technique for meat and fowl as well as for all sorts of fish, such as tuna, red mullet, anchovies and sardines. A North European form is soused herring. In Latin America the pompano fish is often used.*

Serves 6

6 fresh sardines *gutted but heads left on* **(or use fillets of other oily fish such as mackerel, herring, red mullet or even farmed salmon)**

cassava flour (or use fine cornmeal or plain flour)

4 tablespoons olive or sunflower oil

1 onion *finely chopped*

2 garlic cloves *crushed then chopped*

125 ml/4 fl oz red wine vinegar

juice of 1 lime

1 bay leaf

6 black peppercorns

sea salt

1 Wipe the fish, dust with cassava flour and fry in hot oil for about 2 minutes on each side until firm. Remove with a slotted spoon and set aside.

2 In the oil left in the pan, fry the onion over a moderate heat until soft but not brown. Add the garlic and cook for 1 more minute. Pour in the vinegar, 125 ml/4 fl oz water and the lime juice and add the bay leaf and peppercorns. Simmer gently for 10 minutes. Taste and add salt if required.

3 Return the fish to the pan and heat through, then transfer, with the vinegar marinade, to a suitable dish or bowl and leave to cool. Store in the fridge for 24 hours or, preferably, 48 hours before serving. Fish preserved in this way will keep for a month at least if totally immersed in the marinade, with a film of olive or vegetable oil on top, and kept in the fridge in a sealed container.

4 Remove the fish from the marinade to serve.

Cashew Nut Toasts

Torradinhas de Castanho de Cajú

Cashew nuts, the harvest of north-eastern Brazil, are used in many dishes. Here they are the garnish for a typical salgadinho, *or savoury appetizer.* **Serves 6**

1 Preheat the oven to 200°C/400°F/gas 6.

2 Toast the slices of bread, then remove the crusts and cut into quarters.

3 In a bowl mix together the grated cheese, spring onion, paprika and a seasoning of salt and pepper.

4 With a palette knife or other broad-bladed knife, spread the cheese mixture on to the toasts evenly. Arrange on an oiled baking sheet and bake for 10–15 minutes. Once the cheese has melted, remove from the oven and sprinkle with the cashew nuts. Return to the oven to crisp up. Serve hot.

6 slices white bread

125 g/4½ oz mild cheese such as *Minas Gerais* grated (or use crumbled ricotta)

1 tablespoon finely chopped white of spring onion

1 teaspoon paprika

sea salt and freshly ground black pepper

2 tablespoons roughly chopped cashew nuts

Salt Cod Savouries

Bolinhos de Bacalhau

Bacalhau, *or salt cod, is an abiding flavour of Brazil, first introduced by Portuguese colonizers, and ever present on menus today, not least as street food.* **Serves 6**

350 g/12 oz salt cod
cut from the thick part

400 g/14 oz potatoes

2 teaspoons chopped fresh parsley

1 bunch of spring onions, white parts only *finely chopped*

4 free-range eggs *separated*

freshly ground black pepper

plain flour

corn oil for deep-frying

1 Soak the salt cod in cold water overnight, changing the water several times. Put in a saucepan, cover with fresh water and simmer for about 5 minutes, or until soft. Drain. When cool enough to handle, remove the bones carefully and chop the flesh finely.

2 Cook the potatoes whole, in their skins, in boiling salted water. Drain, then peel and mash (not with milk or butter).

3 In a bowl, beat together the mashed potatoes, salt cod, parsley and spring onions. Beat in the egg yolks one at a time until smooth. Season with pepper. If the mixture is slack, add a little flour to make it stiffer.

4 Heat a pan of corn oil to deep-frying temperature (about 180°C/350°F).

5 Whisk the egg whites until stiff and fold into the salt cod mixture.

6 Using a spoon dipped in flour, gently shape spoonfuls of the mixture into balls no larger than an egg. Deep-fry them, a few at a time, for 3–4 minutes or until golden all over. Remove with a slotted spoon and drain on kitchen paper. Serve at once.

Creamy Cod Savouries

Torradinhas de Bacalhau

Torradinha *is the name given to savoury toasts offered as appetizers. These often consist of squares of toast topped with bacon, salami and sausage finished in the oven. Other toppings may be a blob of mayonnaise with a peeled prawn on top or a purée of tuna blended with mayonnaise. This recipe uses a savoury purée of fresh cod with egg. A more pungent version can be made with dried salt cod that has been soaked overnight in several changes of cold water, simmered and the bones carefully removed.* **Serves 6**

1 Preheat the oven to 200°C/400°F/gas 6.

2 Heat the oil in a frying pan and cook the onions gently until soft and changing colour, but not browned.

3 Add the cod steak (or cooked salt cod) with the parsley and cook gently until done, when it will break into flakes. Take the fish from the pan and, when cool enough to handle, remove the bones carefully, together with any skin. Chop the flesh finely. Return to the pan and stir well into the cooked onions. Heat through.

4 Pour in the beaten eggs and season well. Stir until the mixture begins to firm up.

5 Spread out the squares of bread on an oiled baking sheet. Top each with a spoonful of the cod and egg mixture. Bake for 10–15 minutes, or until thoroughly heated and crisp. Serve hot.

3 tablespoons olive oil

2 medium onions *finely chopped*

125 g/4½ oz cod steak or cooked dried salt cod

1 tablespoon chopped fresh parsley

6 free-range eggs *lightly beaten*

sea salt and freshly ground black pepper

6 slices white bread
each cut into four

MAIN DISHES

Black Beans

Feijão

Beans and rice are the universal staples of the Latin-American world, especially in Brazil, the world's major grower of beans. The most popular bean is the small black bean, often known as the turtle bean. Every family has its own way of preparing and flavouring them, adding a little bacon, fried onion, chilli, sausage or tomato to taste. Some beans are always taken out and crushed with a wooden spoon to thicken the sauce. Sometimes all the beans are crushed, to produce a thick purée which is more digestible than the whole beans. Soaking and cooking times for the beans depend on their age; at a good wholefood store with a steady turnover you may expect them to be freshest. **Serves 6–8**

450 g/1 lb dried black beans

chunk of smoked bacon or bacon bone (optional)

1 onion *finely chopped*

55 g/2 oz lard or bacon fat for frying

1 garlic clove *crushed then chopped*

5 cm/2 in piece *lingüiça* **or chorizo**

1 bay leaf

sea salt and freshly ground black pepper

1 Rinse the beans thoroughly and discard any discoloured ones. Soak in water to cover for 6 hours.

2 Tip the beans and their soaking water into a large pan, adding more water to bring the level to 15 cm/6 in above the beans. Do not add salt at this stage as it hardens the beans. Bring to the boil and boil rapidly for 10 minutes, then lower the heat. Simmer for 2–3 hours, or until the beans are soft. If using, add the bacon or bone after 1 hour. When necessary, add boiling water so that the beans do not dry out. The beans are done when you can take one out and crush it to a paste.

3 In a frying pan sauté the onion in the lard or bacon fat for 10 minutes or until lightly coloured. Add the garlic and cook for 1 more minute. Peel the skin from the sausage. Shred the sausage, then add to the pan with the bay leaf and cook with the onion for 5 minutes.

4 Transfer two or three ladles of beans with some of their liquid to the frying pan. Using a wooden spoon, crush the beans to a purée. Season with salt and pepper. Add the bean and sausage mixture to the pan of beans. Cook for at least a further 15 minutes to blend all the flavours.

Mule Drivers' Beans

Feijão de Tropeira

One of three classic bean dishes in Brazil, this is still, believe it or not, cooked by mule drivers plying their timeless trade in the hinterlands of northern Brazil. They would use mulatinho *beans (literally 'mule drivers' beans'), a kind of red kidney bean.* **Serves 6**

1 Soak the beans in cold water overnight. Soak the dried salted beef in another bowl of cold water, changing the water several times; if using bacon, soak it with the beef to remove excess salt.

2 Drain the beans and salted beef and put them in a large pot with the smoked pork or bacon. Cover with fresh water and cook for about 1½–2 hours or until the beans are very tender and easily mashed with a fork. (Cooking times will vary with the freshness of the beans.)

3 In a frying pan, fry the onions in the olive oil until soft and yellow. Add the chopped sausage, crushing with the back of a fork to mash it. Add a few ladlefuls of beans and crush them into the mixture to make a coarse purée. Add this to the pot of cooking beans and cook for a further 10 minutes, although you can leave it on a low heat to simmer for much longer if you wish, topping up with water as required.

4 To serve, remove the chunks of meat, cut into smaller pieces and return to the pot of beans. Garnish with hard-boiled egg slices, chopped parsley and crispy bacon strips.

400 g/14 oz dried red kidney beans

175 g/6 oz chunk dried salted beef (*carne de sol***)**

75 g/3 oz chunk smoked belly of pork or smoked streaky bacon

1 onion *chopped*

1 tablespoon olive oil

175 g/6 oz chorizo or *lingüiça* *chopped*

To garnish:

4 hard-boiled free-range eggs *sliced*

sprig of fresh parsley *chopped*

strips of bacon *fried until crisp*

The National Dish

Feijoada Completa

The most familiar dish in the country, feijoada completa *is the daily staple dressed in its Sunday best or, to be precise, Saturday best, for that is the day it appears on menus throughout Brazil. This dish really needs the small black beans of Brazil,* feijão preto, *and you should use as many varied meats as you can — this recipe includes about 1.5 kg / 3 lb 5 oz in all. Typical accompaniments are steaming white rice, Crispy Stir-fried Kale (page 73), toasted Golden Cassava Flour (page 72),* malagueta *chilli sauce or Chilli Salsa made with some of the bean liquid (page 21) and slices of orange. And, of course, a glass of ice-cold* cachaça, *the spirit made from cane sugar.* **Serves 6**

500 g/1 lb 2 oz dried black beans

500 g/1 lb 2 oz stewing beef (half could be sun-dried salted beef, *carne de sol***)**

2 pig's trotters (plus optional bits such as ears, tail and, especially, salted tongue)

250 g/9 oz smoked pork ribs

175 g/6 oz chunk smoked streaky bacon

1 large tomato *skinned and seeded*

1 tablespoon tomato purée

1 bay leaf

sea salt and freshly ground black pepper

1 onion *finely chopped*

1 tablespoon vegetable oil

175 g/6 oz chorizo *chopped*

2 garlic cloves *crushed then chopped*

bunch of spring onions, white parts only *chopped*

1 fresh green chilli *seeded* **(optional)**

1 Rinse the beans, then soak in water overnight. Soak any salted meats overnight, changing the water several times, to reduce salt content.

2 Use two large pans. Put the drained beans in one pan and the meat (except the chorizo) in the other together with the tomato, tomato purée, bay leaf, salt and pepper. Cover with fresh water and bring to the boil, then turn down to a simmer. Cook for 1 hour (both need skimming in the early stages). Drain the meats and add them to the pan of beans. Continue to cook for 30 minutes, or until the beans are mushy (the beans and meat should cook in about the same time).

3 In a frying pan, cook the onion in the oil until it is soft and golden. Add the chorizo, garlic, spring onions and chilli, if using. Ladle some beans from the cooking pot with their liquid into the frying pan. Mash up well, then add this coarse purée to the bean pan, to thicken the cooking liquid. Simmer for at least 10 minutes to blend the flavours.

4 To serve, remove all the meats, slice each nicely into six pieces, so that each guest will get a variety, and arrange on a large platter. Dribble with some of the cooking liquid to moisten. Serve the beans alongside.

Stuffed Cabbage Parcels

Trouxinhas de Repolho

A dish with a distinctly European touch, similar recipes being found in peasant communities in France, Italy, Spain and Portugal. **Serves 4 as a light lunch course**

12 leaves from a large savoy cabbage *hard core removed*

1 medium onion *chopped*

4 tablespoons olive oil

4 garlic cloves *crushed then chopped*

500 g/1 lb 2 oz minced pork

sea salt and freshly ground black pepper

225 g/8 oz long-grain white rice

250 g/9 oz tomatoes *skinned, seeded and chopped* **or 1 x 400 g/14 oz can whole tomatoes** *drained and seeded, juice reserved*

1 tablespoon tomato purée

1 In a large pan of boiling water, blanch the cabbage leaves for a few minutes to soften. Plunge into cold water, then drain. Set aside.

2 Fry the onion in 2 tablespoons of the olive oil until soft but not brown. Add 3 of the garlic cloves and cook for 1 more minute. Stir in the pork mince and cook until it loses its raw colour. Season. Remove from the heat and leave until cool enough to handle. Mix in the uncooked rice.

3 In a saucepan, fry the remaining garlic in the remaining 2 tablespoons olive oil for 1 minute, without browning. Add the tomatoes, tomato purée and 500 ml/18 fl oz water. (If using canned tomatoes, measure the reserved tomato juice and add enough water to make up the required amount.) Simmer for 5 minutes.

4 Spread out the cabbage leaves on a work surface. Spoon some of the pork and rice mixture into the middle of each leaf and wrap up into a tidy small parcel. Pack into the bottom of a wide saucepan, with the folds underneath.

5 Cover with the tomato sauce and bring to the boil. Turn down the heat, cover with a lid and, preferably using a heat diffuser, simmer gently for 45 minutes. Check the liquid level from time to time to make sure it doesn't dry out or burn, adding a little boiling water as required.

Chopped Rump Steak

Picadinhos de Carne

This is probably the most common meat dish in all Brazil. To make it successfully it is important not to use minced beef or even best minced steak — you need to buy a good cut of rump steak which you then chop to a minced texture. This will retain the juiciness of the meat. Don't use a food processor or a mincer to grind the meat as they squeeze out all the liquid content, giving the meat a cardboard-like texture when cooked. Serve with Brazilian Rice (page 76) and peas. **Serves 4**

1 Trim the steak to remove fat and any gristle. Using a sharp, broad-bladed knife on a chopping board, chop the steak finely to a minced texture. It is a matter of taste how finely you chop the meat — the finer it is, the richer the sauce; the thicker it is, the juicier the meat.

2 In a frying pan, heat a film of olive oil and fry the bacon until the fat runs. Add the onion and fry until soft but not brown.

3 Add the chopped steak and stir over the heat until it changes colour. Season. Stir in the tomatoes and cook for a few more minutes. Pour in enough water to cover and simmer for 30 minutes, stirring from time to time, until the meat is well cooked and the sauce is a thick reduction. Add more water if it becomes too dry.

750 g/1 lb 10 oz rump steak

olive oil for frying

100 g/3½ oz best streaky bacon *cut into dice*

1 onion *finely chopped*

sea salt and freshly ground black pepper

250 g/9 oz tomatoes *skinned, seeded and chopped*

Meatballs in Tomato Sauce

Almondegas com Molho de Tomate

São Paulo, with its huge immigrant community, may owe this dish to the Italians who were first to settle there, back in the 1860s. It is an abiding favourite that has stood the test of time. You can use pork, or even lamb or chicken, instead of beef. **Serves 4–6**

1 Crumble the bread into a bowl and moisten with the milk. With a wooden spoon, beat in the eggs to produce a smooth paste.

2 Add the beef, onion, garlic and a seasoning of salt and pepper. With your hands, mix well together and then shape the mixture into even-sized balls, no more than 5 cm/2 in in diameter. Dust the meatballs with flour.

3 Pour enough oil into a large frying pan to cover the bottom and get it very hot. Fry the meatballs, in several batches if necessary, until well browned all over. Remove with a slotted spoon and drain on kitchen paper. Set aside.

4 Discard the fat and wipe out the pan, then cook the onion and garlic in a knob of butter for a few minutes or until soft. Add the tomatoes, the tomato purée and seasoning. Cook until the mixture thickens, stirring to prevent sticking. Check the seasoning, then add the meatballs to the tomato sauce and cook together for a further 10 minutes.

5 Serve with steaming hot, boiled white rice.

4 slices white bread *crusts removed*

125 ml/4 fl oz milk

2 free-range eggs

1 kg/2¼ lb finely minced beef or veal

1 large onion *chopped*

3 garlic cloves *crushed*

sea salt and freshly ground black pepper

plain flour

oil for frying

For the sauce:

1 large onion *grated*

2 garlic cloves *crushed*

butter for frying

750 g/1 lb 10 oz tomatoes *skinned, seeded and chopped* **or**
2 x 400 g/14 oz cans whole tomatoes *drained and chopped*

2 teaspoons tomato purée

To serve:

boiled long-grain white rice

Barbecued Meats

Churrasco à Gaucho

The churrascaria *is a barbecue, and is particularly popular in the south, where there is plenty of meat. Whenever possible, large cuts of meat are roasted on a spit over the barbecue and then divided after cooking. Unique to Brazil is the method of rinsing the meat with brine as it cooks — this prevents the surface from hardening to the point where it can form a shield against heat penetration. Brazilians do not cut off fat from meat before grilling, for this both aids the cooking and adds to the flavour. Cut away surplus after cooking, by all means. For a party, the host will cook many cuts and types of meat, including chicken, pork, offal and, especially, sausages. White meats — chicken and pork — are always marinated first, in a mixture of lime juice, finely chopped onion and garlic, chopped parsley or coriander and seasoning to taste. Mop the meat dry before grilling.* **Serves 4**

1 teaspoon coarse sea salt

1 kg/2¼ lb rump steak, sirloin or beef fillet in one piece

1 Dissolve the salt in 100 ml/3½ fl oz boiling water to make the brine for basting.

2 Make the fire in the barbecue. When the charcoal embers are red hot and the flames have died down, skewer the meat and put it in place over the charcoal.

3 Grill for 5 minutes on each side, occasionally brushing with the brine solution (use a pastry brush or, in more bucolic vein, a sprig of fresh rosemary or thyme). If the meat is cooked longer it will dry out and harden, but some prefer it so.

4 Remove the meat from the heat and leave to rest for a few minutes before slicing. Serve accompanied by salads, boiled long-grain white rice, Golden Cassava Flour (page 72) and a Chilli Salsa (page 21).

Dried Beef Purée

Paçoca

Paçoca (pronounced pass-occa) is one of the chief dishes of Pernambuco in the very north of Brazil, where the climate does not look kindly on the raising of cattle. Hence the most common form of meat is carne de sol, *or salted meat (often the breast) dried in the sun.* Carne de sol *needs to be soaked to draw out the salt before cooking, after which it is pounded (another version of this meat when cooked is* velha roupa — *literally old rags, which is what the meat resembles when treated in this way). For paçoca, the cooked meat is mixed with cassava flour to make a nourishing and solid purée. In place of* carne de sol *you can use a cut of salt beef from a butcher.* **Serves 4–6**

1 Soak the dried salted beef in water to cover for 4–6 hours to draw out the salt, changing the water several times. Drain and mop dry. Cut into cubes about 2.5 cm/1 in across.

2 Cut the belly of pork into small dice. Cook them in a large frying pan over a low heat until the fat runs. Add the beef and cook until golden brown. Remove the pork and beef with a slotted spoon and set aside. Using the same fat, cook the onions until soft and golden.

3 Combine the meat and onions and pound them in a mortar, to break up the meat into shreds. Or use a food processor, but don't overdo it.

4 Mix in the cassava flour gradually, to make a dense, smooth purée. Return to the frying pan and heat through, stirring. Season to taste. Serve hot with boiled rice.

500 g/1 lb 2 oz dried salted beef (*carne de sol*)

250 g /9 oz belly of pork

4 onions *chopped*

1 kg/2¼ lb cassava flour

sea salt and freshly ground black pepper

To serve:

boiled long-grain white rice

Chicken and Prawn Stew

Xinxim

Combining fowl and shellfish is typical of the cooking of northern Brazil. This classic dish is seasoned with dried prawns and thickened with nuts. It is traditionally served with white rice, Coconut and Prawn Cream (page 79), Golden Cassava Flour (page 72) and a chilli sauce. Dried prawns, although typical, have a pungent smell and can be omitted. **Serves 4**

1.5 kg/3 lb 5 oz chicken *cut into 8 joints*

juice of 3 limes

3 garlic cloves *crushed then chopped*

sea salt and freshly ground black pepper

250 g/9 oz peeled raw prawns

sunflower oil for frying

1 onion *finely chopped*

1 green pepper *seeded and finely chopped*

2 large tomatoes *skinned, seeded and chopped*

250 ml/9 fl oz chicken stock

30 g/1 oz dried prawns

30 g/1 oz cashew nuts

30 g/1 oz shelled peanuts *toasted and skins rubbed off*

1 cm/½ in piece fresh ginger *peeled and grated*

2 tablespoons *dendê* oil

125 ml/4 fl oz first pressing coconut milk (see page 13)

sprig of fresh coriander

1 Put the chicken pieces in a bowl, add one-third of the lime juice and garlic and season. Toss, then leave to marinate for 30 minutes. In another bowl, mix together half of the fresh prawns, half of the remaining lime juice and garlic and seasoning and leave to marinate for 15 minutes.

2 Dry the prawns with kitchen paper, then fry in 1 tablespoon of oil for a few minutes on each side or until pink. Remove and reserve. Add a little more oil to the pan, then dry the chicken pieces and fry until golden on each side. Remove and reserve.

3 Clean the pan, add a little fresh oil and fry the onion until soft but not brown. Add the green pepper and cook until it softens. Add the rest of the garlic and cook for 1 more minute without letting it brown. Add the tomatoes and heat through, then return the chicken pieces. Cover with the stock, bring to the boil then cover and simmer for 30 minutes, checking occasionally to make sure the chicken isn't sticking and that the liquid hasn't boiled dry (add a little boiling water if necessary).

4 With a pestle and mortar, or in an electric grinder, grind the dried prawns and nuts to a powder. Stir into the chicken mixture together with the grated ginger. Heat through for 5 minutes, then check the seasoning.

5 Add the cooked prawns, remaining lime juice, *dendê* oil and coconut milk and heat through. Serve hot, garnished with coriander.

Fish in Coconut Milk

Peixe ao Leite de Côco

This is one of the most typical ways of cooking fish in Brazil, and is used with almost every variety. The fish is usually marinated in this fashion. **Serves 4**

4 steaks of white fish such as cod (about 250 g/9 oz each)

1 onion *diced small*

2 green peppers *seeded and diced*

2 tomatoes *skinned, seeded and diced*

150 ml/¼ pint coconut milk (see page 13)

1 tablespoon tomato purée

1 tablespoon olive oil

For the marinade:

juice of 2 limes

2 garlic cloves *crushed then chopped*

2 sprigs of fresh coriander *chopped*

sea salt

1 Put the fish steaks in a bowl and add the ingredients for the marinade. Mix, then leave to marinate for 30 minutes.

2 Transfer the fish steaks and the marinade to a large pan, arranging them in one layer, and cover with the onion, green peppers and tomatoes. Mix the coconut milk with the tomato purée and pour over the fish. Sprinkle with the olive oil and leave to sit for 15 minutes to allow the fish to absorb the flavours.

3 Set the pan over a low heat and simmer for 25 minutes. Brazilians do not mind the fact that the fish becomes very firm when cooked in this way. If more tender fish is preferred, remove the fish from the pan after it has been sitting for 15 minutes and simmer the other ingredients for 15 minutes. Then put the fish back into the coconut milk mixture to cook for 10–15 minutes.

Prawn Stew
Moqueca de Camarão

Moqueca (pronounced mok-ekka) is the simple stew of the north, in which fresh sliced vegetables are stewed slowly in oil for 20 minutes before prawns, fish or other ingredients are added. The most authentic versions contain too much rich dendê oil for non-Brazilian palates, so this recipe substitutes vegetable oil (use sunflower or groundnut oil, or even olive oil), with a little dendê oil to finish, thus supplying both the typical orange colour and distinctive flavour. **Serves 4**

1 Simmer the vegetables in the oil over a low heat until they soften and release their juices, about 20 minutes. Season to taste.

2 Add the prawns and simmer for a further 5 minutes, shaking to ensure even cooking. Avoid overcooking. Add the *dendê* oil and stir.

3 Serve hot with plain white rice, and a bowl each of Chilli Salsa and *malagueta* chilli.

2 large tomatoes *skinned, seeded and sliced*

2 peppers (1 red and 1 green) *seeded and thinly sliced*

1 large mild onion *thinly sliced lengthways*

100 ml /3½ fl oz olive oil

sea salt and freshly ground black pepper

700 g/1 lb 9 oz peeled raw prawns

4 tablespoons *dendê* oil

To serve:

boiled long-grain white rice

Chilli Salsa (see page 21)

***malagueta* chilli**

Stuffed Crabs

Casquinhos Recheados

This is one of the most popular dishes from northern Brazil, where seafood is abundant. It is commonly made with smallish crabs, about 7.5 cm / 3 in across, but this is not vital for success. **Serves 4**

1 Mix the lime juice with the crab meat, both white and brown, and season with salt and pepper. Leave to marinate for 30 minutes.

2 Cook the onion gently in the oil until it softens. Add the crab meat, tomatoes, parsley and Tabasco. Cook for a few minutes to blend the flavours, stirring and moistening with a little water to prevent it from sticking. Stir in the cornflour mixture and continue cooking for a few more minutes to thicken.

3 Preheat the oven to 200°C/400°F/gas 6.

4 Fill the scrubbed crab shells with the crab meat stuffing and sprinkle with the grated cheese. Set on a baking tray and bake for 10 minutes or until the cheese begins to bubble and brown. Serve at once.

juice of 2 limes

4 medium-sized crabs *meat removed and shells retained*

sea salt and freshly ground black pepper

1 onion *finely chopped*

4 tablespoons sunflower oil

2 large tomatoes *skinned, seeded and chopped*

sprig of fresh parsley *chopped*

splash of Tabasco or chilli sauce

1 teaspoon cornflour *mixed with 1 tablespoon cold water*

125 g/4½ oz Parmesan or Cheddar cheese *grated*

Prawn Frittata

Frigideira de Camarão

This is similar to the Italian frittata of oven-baked scrambled eggs. A frigideira *though, in spite of the way it sounds, is not a cold dish, the* frigideira *being a heavy iron frying pan which can be used equally on top of the stove or in the oven. Unusually, baking powder is mixed with the beaten eggs. A deliciously savoury* frigideira *is also made with salt cod (de-salted by soaking overnight), cooked as below, or rehydrated* carne de sol *(salted dried meat) or even green cashew nuts.* **Serves 4**

500 g/1 lb 2 oz peeled raw prawns

1 onion *finely chopped*

1 green pepper *seeded and diced*

olive oil for frying

1 large tomato *skinned, seeded and diced*

2 sprigs of fresh coriander *chopped*

3 tablespoons first pressing coconut milk (see page 13)

butter for greasing

6 free-range eggs

½ teaspoon baking powder

For the marinade:

juice of 1 lime

2 garlic cloves *crushed then chopped*

sea salt and freshly ground black pepper

To serve:

boiled long-grain white rice

1 Preheat the oven to 190°C/375°F/gas 5.

2 Marinate the prawns in the lime juice, garlic, salt and pepper for 30 minutes.

3 Fry the onion and green pepper in a little olive oil until soft. Add the tomato, coriander and coconut milk and simmer until the mixture begins to thicken.

4 Stir in the prawns and heat through to incorporate the flavours.

5 Butter an oven dish of a suitable size (unless you have used an ovenproof iron frying pan) and transfer the prawn mixture to it. Beat the eggs with the baking powder, adding salt to taste, and pour over the prawns. Bake for 30–40 minutes or until set.

6 Serve with steaming hot boiled white rice.

Mussel Stew
Moqueca de Sururú

This is a dish familiar the world over, but, inevitably, in Brazil it is enhanced by the sweet and sour flavours of coconut milk and lime juice. **Serves 4**

I kg/2¼ lb mussels

200 g/7 oz onion *thinly sliced*

200 g/7 oz tomatoes *skinned, seeded and sliced*

4 sprigs of fresh coriander *chopped*

2 garlic cloves *crushed then chopped*

juice of 2 limes

200 ml/7 fl oz coconut milk (see page 13)

100 ml/3½ fl oz *dendê* oil (or use olive oil)

sea salt and freshly ground black pepper

To serve:

boiled long-grain white rice

Golden Cassava Flour (see page 72)

1 Rinse the mussels in cold water, discarding any that are open (they are dead), broken or heavy (they may contain mud). If necessary, scrub with a brush. Holding the shells firmly between thumb and forefinger, tug off the hairy 'beards'.

2 Put the mussels in a large saucepan and add the onion, tomato, coriander, garlic, lime juice, coconut milk, oil and a seasoning of salt and pepper (when adding salt, allow for the fact that the liquor that will come from the mussels when they open is salty).

3 Put the pan on a fierce heat, cover with a lid and cook rapidly until the mussels open — a matter of only a few minutes if the pan is sufficiently hot.

4 Serve in bowls accompanied by steaming hot plain boiled rice and toasted cassava flour.

Okra and Peanut Stew

Caruru

Caruru, from the north-east, is one of the most African and most traditional of Brazilian dishes. It combines okra with both dried and fresh prawns, and a thickening of peanuts and cashew nuts, to make a tasty, glutinous dish to serve with Coconut Rice (page 77). The dish is richer if you use fish stock rather than water. If you are peeling your own prawns, reserve the shells and use them to make a stock: fry them lightly in a little butter or oil, then simmer them, just covered with water, with ½ chopped onion, 1 garlic clove, a bay leaf, a few peppercorns, a pinch of paprika and some fresh coriander stems for 15 minutes; strain, squeezing all the juices from the shells. You can, of course, make a stock with fish bones instead of prawn shells. Note that dried prawns are very pungent, and although authentic, can be omitted. **Serves 4–6**

1 Trim the okra and chop into very small pieces. Sprinkle with the lemon juice and a little salt.

2 In a food processor (or with a pestle and mortar) first grind the nuts, and then the dried prawns.

3 Heat the oil in a large frying pan and cook the onion on a moderate heat until it starts to turn yellow. Stir in the ground dried prawns and nuts and cook for a few more minutes.

4 Add the whole prawns and the ginger and cook for a few minutes, then add the fish stock or water and the okra. Simmer for 30 minutes on the lowest heat, stirring to prevent sticking and adding more water to avoid it drying out.

5 Depending on your tastes, add a few drops of *pimenta-de-cheiro* or a chilli sauce such as Tabasco diluted with a little boiling water. Sprinkle with toasted cassava flour and serve with coconut rice.

1 kg/2¼ lb okra

juice of 1 lemon

sea salt and freshly ground black pepper

100 g/3½ oz shelled peanuts (or use 55 g/2 oz peanuts and 40 g/1½ oz cashew nuts) *lightly toasted and skins rubbed off*

125 g/4½ oz dried prawns *chopped*

2 tablespoons *dendê* oil (or use sunflower oil)

1 onion *finely chopped*

500 g/1 lb 2 oz peeled raw prawns

1 teaspoon grated fresh ginger

250 ml/9 fl oz fish stock or water

***pimenta-de-cheiro* pickled in vinegar (or use Tabasco sauce)**

Golden Cassava Flour (see page 72)

Coconut Rice (see page 77)

Shellfish Savoury Rice

Arroz de Marisco

This typical rice dish from the north has neither the sophistication of an Italian seafood risotto nor the intensity of a Spanish arroz marinera *in which seafood flavours are absorbed while the rice is cooking. On the other hand it has the merits of simplicity, depending mainly on the excellence of the shellfish used.* **Serves 4**

1 Put the prawns and crab meat in a bowl, and toss with half the lime juice, the coriander and a seasoning of salt and pepper.

2 In a frying pan, sauté the onion in a little olive oil until soft. Stir in the tomato and tomato purée. Add the prawns and crab meat and, when very hot, add the mussels and oysters (or clams). Cover and cook until all the shells open in the steam, which will take only a few minutes.

3 Add the rest of the lime juice and check seasoning. Stir in the cooked rice and heat through until it is steaming and has absorbed the flavours of the seafood.

250 g/9 oz peeled raw prawns

250 g/9 oz white crab meat

juice of 2 limes

3 sprigs of fresh coriander *chopped*

sea salt and freshly ground black pepper

1 onion *finely chopped*

olive oil for frying

1 large tomato *skinned and seeded*

1 teaspoon tomato purée

20 mussels *scrubbed and bearded*

4 or 8 fresh oysters or clams in shell

500 g/1 lb 2 oz long-grain white rice *boiled and left to cool*

SIDE
DISHES

Purée of Brown Beans

Tutú à Mineira

This is the predominant dish of the Minas Gerais province where it's eaten with all pork dishes, alongside plain white rice and the universal couve *greens (Crispy Stir-fried Kale, page 73). You don't need a lot of dried beans, because they double in size as they soak.*
Serves up to 6

1 Put the beans in a saucepan and cover with fresh water. Bring to the boil, skimming off the scum that rises to the surface. (Don't add salt at this stage as it would harden the beans.) Turn down the heat and simmer for about 2 hours, or until tender. Beans vary in cooking time with quality and age, so cook longer if still hard.

2 Meanwhile, in a frying pan, cook the onion in the oil until soft. Add the green pepper and cook for a further 5 minutes. Add the garlic and cook for 1 minute. Stir in the tomatoes and cook for a few more minutes. Stir in the cassava flour together with 500 ml / 18 fl oz of the liquid the beans are cooking in. Mix to a smooth paste, adding seasoning to taste.

3 Using a slotted spoon, remove the beans from their cooking liquid (which you must reserve). Purée them in a blender, in batches, adding a little of the reserved liquid to make a smooth purée.

4 In a large pan, mix together the puréed beans and the cassava flour mixture, adding enough bean cooking liquid to give a texture that is neither too stiff nor too soupy. Check the seasoning. Stand this pan in a larger pan of simmering water to prevent burning or sticking. Heat for 15 minutes so the flavours blend and the mixture thickens. You can leave it to simmer for longer, but top up with liquid as necessary.

5 Serve sprinkled with chopped coriander and spring onions.

250 g/9 oz dried small Brazilian brown beans (or use kidney beans) *soaked overnight*

1 onion *finely chopped*

2 tablespoons olive or sunflower oil

1 green pepper *seeded and chopped*

2 garlic cloves *crushed then chopped*

2 tomatoes *skinned, seeded and chopped*

75 g/3 oz cassava flour

sea salt and freshly ground black pepper

To serve:

sprig of fresh coriander *finely chopped*

bunch of spring onions *chopped*

Golden Cassava Flour

Farofa Amarela

The most widely used garnish in Brazil, this is sprinkled like toasted breadcrumbs on meat dishes such as stews, Barbecued Meats (page 52) and the National Dish (page 46). It has a nutty, appetizing taste. In the north it mops up the savoury gravies of fish stews such as mussel moqueca (page 64). Farofa amarela (also called farofa mantiega) is made from coarsely refined cassava flour that is toasted to a golden brown with a little dendê oil or butter to give it a yellow colour. It is simply served in a saucer at the table for you to help yourself. Ambitious cooks often add other ingredients appropriate to what they are serving, such as frying shreds of streaky bacon first, then cooking the cassava flour in the resulting fat. Cassava flour may be toasted with a beaten egg, which causes it to thicken into small lumps. Chopped raw onion may be added, or herbs with roast pork, or sliced bananas and dried fruit with a seafood dish, or ground dried prawns as in the variation below. **Serves 6**

225 g/8 oz cassava flour

pinch of sea salt

3 tablespoons *dendê* oil
or 55 g/2 oz butter

1 Heat a frying pan over a moderate heat. Add the cassava flour and salt and stir with a wooden spoon until hot.

2 Stir in the *dendê* oil or butter and cook, stirring, for a few minutes, or until the flour turns golden. Immediately tip it on to a cool plate to stop the toasting process.

Savoury Cassava Flour

This is a more savoury farofa to serve with a Bahian seafood stew or shellfish dish. In a frying pan briskly cook 75 g/3 oz very finely chopped onion in 4 tablespoons dendê oil (or other oil or butter) for 5 minutes to soften it, stirring to prevent it from burning. Mix in 225 g/8 oz cassava flour and 30 g/1 oz ground dried prawns and stir together well, cooking until the cassava flour takes on a golden colour. Remove to a serving plate or saucer. Note that to some tastes dried prawns can be very pungent.

Crispy Stir-fried Kale

Couve

This bright green vegetable is an essential accompaniment to The National Dish (feijoada completa, page 46). Quick cooking to keep its bright colour is important, as is the way it is finely shredded to retain a chewy texture. **Serves 6**

1 Cut out the hard stalks of the kale. Lay the flat leaves on top of each other and roll into a tight wad. Using a broad-bladed knife, cut across the roll into shreds no more than 5 mm/¼ in wide.

2 Heat the oil in a large frying pan or, better still, a wok and stir-fry the shredded leaves rapidly until tender but still chewy. They should keep their bright green colour. Season to taste and serve.

450 g/1 lb curly kale (or use spring greens or Savoy cabbage)

2 tablespoons sunflower oil

sea salt and freshly ground black pepper

Stewed Green Papaya

Refogadinho de Mamão Verde

The mamão *is a larger version of a papaya, with brilliant orange flesh. Unripe, it can be cooked as a vegetable, gently stewed, which is what* refogadinho *means. You can use unripe papaya if you can't get* mamão. **Serves 4**

**1 large *mamão*
(or use 2 green papayas)**

1 onion *chopped*

oil for frying

2 garlic cloves *crushed then chopped*

2 teaspoons tomato purée

**sea salt and freshly ground
black pepper**

1 Peel the skin from the *mamão* or papaya, cut in half and remove the large black seeds from the centre. Prick the flesh with a fork and leave to soak in a bowl of water for 1 hour to remove some of the astringency in the flavour. Drain and reserve.

2 In a frying pan sauté the onion in a little oil until soft and turning golden. Add the garlic and cook for another minute. Stir in the tomato purée and seasoning.

3 Cut the *mamão* or papaya into 2.5 cm/1 in pieces. Stir into the mixture in the pan, cover and simmer for 5 minutes. Serve as a vegetable accompaniment with meat or chicken.

Brazilian Rice

Arroz a Brasileira

Plain boiled rice is the usual accompaniment for beans, but seasoned rice is often served. This is a typical dish. In Brazil rice is not cooked drowning in water, but with just the right amount that will be totally absorbed. A rule of thumb is to use twice the volume of water to rice, e.g. two cups of water to one cup of rice. **Serves 4**

2 tablespoons sunflower oil

1 medium onion *finely chopped*

1 garlic clove *crushed*

250 g/9 oz tomatoes *skinned and seeded* **or 1 x 400 g/14 oz can whole tomatoes** *drained and seeded*

3 sprigs of fresh coriander or parsley *chopped*

sea salt and freshly ground black pepper

450 g/1 lb long-grain white rice

1 In a frying pan, heat the oil until very hot. Add the onion, turn down the heat and fry until it starts to colour. Add the garlic and cook for 1 more minute without colouring.

2 Add the tomatoes, chopped herbs and seasoning and cook rapidly to evaporate excess moisture. Stir in the rice until well mixed.

3 Transfer to a saucepan. Add 1 litre/1¾ pints water and bring to the boil. Then put on the lid (a crumpled piece of foil under the lid will stop steam escaping), turn to the lowest heat and cook for 15 minutes. Use a heat diffuser to prevent burning, if necessary.

4 Remove from the heat and leave, still covered, for 10 minutes to continue cooking in its own steam, allowing the grains to separate. Remove the lid and allow the rice to dry out for a few more minutes before serving.

Coconut Rice

Arroz de Côco

This rice dish is eaten every day in many parts of Brazil to accompany meat, fish or beans. You can use coconut milk that is freshly made, canned coconut milk or that reconstituted from a powder. Alternatively, use 2 tablespoons grated from a bar of compressed coconut.

Serves 4

1 Bring 1 litre/1¾ pints water to the boil, add the rice and salt to taste and simmer with the lid off for 20 minutes.

2 Stir in the coconut milk and cook for a further 5 minutes, when all excess water should be absorbed or evaporated.

450 g/1 lb long-grain white rice

sea salt

4 tablespoons coconut milk (see page 13)

Coconut and Prawn Cream

Vatapá

This is one of the national dishes of Brazil, combining the savoury flavours of prawns with smooth, sweet coconut and hot chilli. It is bound together with crushed roasted almonds, cashew or peanuts. Vatapá may be thickened with cassava flour or cornmeal, but it is more delicate if breadcrumbs are used. If dried prawns are too pungent for your taste, use 225 g/ 8 oz peeled fresh prawns and a few drops of Thai fish sauce (nam pla). **Serves 6**

1 Soak the breadcrumbs in the first pressing coconut milk for 30 minutes, then squeeze together to make a pulp.

2 Soak the dried prawns in water to cover for 30 minutes. Drain and chop.

3 Heat a little oil in a frying pan and fry the onions over a moderate heat for about 10 minutes or until starting to colour. Add the garlic and cook for 1 more minute without colouring.

4 In a blender or food processor (or electric coffee grinder) grind the nuts to a smooth paste. Remove and then purée the dried prawns with the green chillies. Add the ground nuts and the prawn and chilli purée to the frying pan and fry with the onions for a few minutes, stirring well. Add the bay leaf, lime juice and seasoning.

5 Pour in the second pressing coconut milk and the fish stock, if using (you may not need to add all the liquid). Simmer, preferably over a heat diffuser, for 15 minutes or until thickened. Add the thick coconut cream and breadcrumbs at the end, just heating through.

6 For a more substantial dish, add fish and/or prawns, heating through until cooked.

30 g/1 oz breadcrumbs from a day-old white loaf

70 ml/2½ fl oz first pressing coconut milk (see page 13)

125 g/4½ oz dried prawns

***dendê* oil (or use olive oil) for frying**

2 onions *finely chopped*

2 garlic cloves *finely chopped*

250 g/9 oz mixed peeled almonds and cashews (half and half) or all roasted peanuts *skins rubbed off*

2 fresh green chillies *seeded and finely chopped*

1 bay leaf

lime juice

sea salt and freshly ground black pepper

600 ml/1 pint second pressing coconut milk (see page 13)

300 ml/½ pint fish stock (optional)

2 fillets white fish, cooked and flaked (optional)

12 peeled cooked prawns (optional)

79

Prawn and Yam Purée
Bobó de Camarão

This smooth purée, coloured bright orange due to the dendê *oil it is cooked in, is served on its own or as an accompaniment to meat or fish. It has its origins in Nigeria and it is associated with a form of voodoo known as Candomblé. Bobó, also known as* abobó, *can be made with yams (as here), cassava, breadfruit or white beans. The use of cream makes it more luxurious. It is sometimes finished with a dusting of powdered dried prawns that have been toasted in a dry frying pan.* **Serves 4**

750 g/1 lb 10 oz yams *peeled*

1 onion *grated*

***dendê* oil (or use olive oil)**

2 garlic cloves *crushed then chopped*

2.5 cm/1 in piece fresh ginger *peeled and grated*

8 large raw prawns (750 g/ 1 lb 10 oz) *peeled and heads removed*

450 g/1 lb tomatoes *skinned, seeded and chopped* **or 1 x 400 g/14 oz can whole tomatoes** *drained and seeded*

1 teaspoon tomato purée

200 ml/7 fl oz coconut milk (see page 13)

1 tablespoon chopped fresh coriander or parsley

freshly ground black pepper

4 tablespoons double cream (optional)

1 Cut the yam into 6 or 8 pieces. Cook in boiling water for about 20 minutes or until tender (test with a skewer). Remove with a slotted spoon to drain in a colander, reserving the cooking water.

2 When cool, purée the yam in batches in a blender (or use a potato ricer). Add a little of the cooking liquid if the mixture is too stiff. Set aside.

3 In a non-stick frying pan, fry the onion in a little oil on a moderate heat until soft. Add the garlic and ginger and fry for 1 more minute. Add the prawns and cook for 2 minutes on each side, or until pink and opaque. Remove and reserve the prawns.

4 Add the tomatoes, tomato purée, coconut milk, coriander and pepper to taste to the pan. Simmer uncovered for 15 minutes, or until some of the moisture evaporates. Stir occasionally to prevent sticking.

5 Add the yam purée and cook for a few more minutes, stirring to a smooth consistency. Fold in the prawns and, when hot, remove from the heat and stir in the cream.

Banana Bread

Pão de Banana

One of the delights of staying at an international hotel in Brazil is the promise of a breakfast feast. There is nothing grudging about the range of treats on offer, both savoury and sweet, from fresh tropical fruit to savoury specials, pastries, puddings, cakes and fruit breads, none more delightful than banana bread. Yeast is not part of the baking tradition in Brazil and many breads are made with baking powder as this one is. **Makes 1 loaf**

1 Preheat the oven to 180°C/350°F/gas 4.

2 In a bowl, cream the butter with the sugar until thick and fluffy, then beat in the egg thoroughly.

3 In another bowl mix the flour with the baking powder, salt and nutmeg.

4 Mix some of the mashed banana and the vanilla essence into the egg and butter mixture, beating well. Then beat in some of the flour mixture. Continue adding the banana and the flour mixture alternately until everything is beaten in. Stir in the raisins and nuts.

5 Pour into a greased loaf tin that measures 23 x 12.5 cm/9 x 5 in. Bake for 1 hour. Test if the bread is cooked by inserting a metal skewer into the centre: it should come out clean. Leave to cool in the tin for 15 minutes before turning out on to a wire rack.

125 g/4½ oz unsalted butter *at room temperature*

2 tablespoons caster sugar

1 free-range egg *beaten*

250 g/9 oz plain white flour

1 tablespoon baking powder

pinch of salt

½ teaspoon grated nutmeg

3 large ripe bananas *mashed*

½ teaspoon pure vanilla essence

100 g/3½ oz seedless raisins *dusted in flour*

3 tablespoons roughly chopped nuts (such as Brazil nuts or pecans)

Fried Plantains

Banana Comprida Frita

Plantains look like bananas and they are related, but they never ripen or sweeten, even when the skin changes colour from green to black. As a starchy alternative to potatoes, they make excellent chips. They are also used in soups and sweetened to make a dessert. **Serves 4**

2 large plantains

oil or clarified butter for frying

1 It is not as easy to peel a plantain as a banana. Cut off the ends, then run the tip of a sharp knife along the ridges and pull the peel away. Cut the plantains in two, and divide each half into four, cutting lengthways to make long chips.

2 Shallow fry in oil or clarified butter for a few minutes on each side until nicely browned. Serve hot.

Cheese Rolls

Pão de Queijo

The most universal, almost the most popular, form of bread, this is found everywhere. Some rolls are made with wheat flour, but this feather-light version uses tapioca flour, derived from the roots of the cassava plant. **Makes 12**

1 Preheat the oven to 230°C/450°F/gas 8.

2 Sift the tapioca flour into a bowl. In a saucepan, combine the oil and salt with 80 ml/3 fl oz water and bring to the boil. Slowly pour on to the tapioca, stirring it to a stiff dough with a wooden spoon.

3 When the dough has cooled slightly, stir in the egg, then the yogurt and, finally, the cheese.

4 Grease your hands with an oily piece of kitchen paper, then form the dough into 12 balls. Arrange them on a non-stick baking sheet. Put into the oven and immediately reduce the temperature to 180°C/350°F/gas 4. Bake for 25–30 minutes. You should be able to tell that the rolls are done by the appetizing smell, but you can test for doneness by inserting a skewer – if it comes out clean they are ready. Cool on a wire rack.

225 g/8 oz tapioca flour

50 ml/2 fl oz sunflower oil

generous pinch of sea salt

1 free-range egg *beaten*

6 tablespoons plain yogurt

55 g/2 oz hard cheese, preferably Parmesan *freshly grated*

Coconut Bread

Pão de Côco

Another tasty breakfast bread, but quite dense, this has the appearance of a flat cake.
Makes 2 loaves

350 g/12 oz plain white flour

1 tablespoon baking powder

1 teaspoon salt

250 g/9 oz freshly grated coconut

80 ml/3 fl oz evaporated milk

1 free-range egg *beaten*

125 g/4½ oz butter *melted and cooled*

125 g/4½ oz caster sugar

½ teaspoon pure vanilla essence

1 Preheat the oven to 180°C/350°F/gas 4.

2 Put the flour, baking powder and salt into a large bowl and mix in the grated coconut.

3 Whisk the evaporated milk with the egg, melted butter, sugar and vanilla essence until evenly mixed. Scoop out a well in the centre of the flour and coconut mixture and pour in the liquid. Beat well together to make a soft mixture.

4 Divide the mixture between 2 buttered loaf tins, each measuring 23 x 12.5 cm/9 x 5 in, filling them half-way. Bake for 50 minutes to 1 hour. Test if the bread is cooked by inserting a metal skewer into the centre: it should not be sticky when you draw it out.

5 Remove from the oven and leave to cool in the tins for 10 minutes. Then turn out on to a wire rack to finish cooling.

Sweet Coconut Cornbread

Pão de Milho com Côco

The flavour of this cornbread is enhanced by the inclusion of grated coconut and coconut milk. **Makes 2 loaves**

1 Preheat the oven to 180°C/350°F/gas 4.

2 In a large bowl, mix together the cornmeal, flour, sugar, salt, baking powder and spices.

3 Whisk the eggs, milk, coconut milk and butter together in another bowl. Gradually stir the liquid into the dry ingredients. Fold in the grated coconut, dried fruit and candied peel mixture, and lime zest.

4 Spoon the mixture into 2 greased loaf tins, each measuring 23 x 12.5 cm/9 x 5 in. Bake for 35–45 minutes. Test if the bread is cooked by inserting a skewer into the centre: it should come out clean. Leave to cool in the tin for 15 minutes before turning out on to a wire rack.

350 g/12 oz yellow cornmeal (maize meal)

125 g/4½ oz plain white flour

2 tablespoons caster sugar

1 teaspoon salt

2 tablespoons baking powder

½ teaspoon each ground cinnamon, cloves and grated nutmeg

4 free-range eggs *well beaten*

8 tablespoons milk

8 tablespoons coconut milk (see page 13)

175 g/6 oz butter *melted*

250 g/9 oz freshly grated coconut (approximately 2 coconuts)

250 g/9 oz mixed dried fruit (such as currants, raisins, sultanas) and candied peel *dusted with flour*

grated zest of 1 lime

Chayote Salad with Oranges

Salada de Xuxu

Among the most popular ingredients for salad is the chayote or xuxu *(pronounced shoe-shoe). It's a hard-skinned vegetable that's as green as a Granny Smith, and probably thinks it's a fruit as it has large edible white pips inside. It's bland to the taste, but what it lacks in flavour it makes up for with its fresh, juicy texture. Chayotes combine well with other vegetables and fruits, especially those with acidic flavours.* **Serves 4**

2 chayotes *peeled, seeded and shredded on a grater*

3 oranges *peeled and segmented (juice reserved)*

bunch of spring onions, white parts only *chopped*

1 tablespoon extra virgin olive oil

juice of 2 limes

sea salt and freshly ground black pepper

To serve:

3 sprigs of fresh coriander, parsley or mint *chopped*

1 Mix the grated chayote with the orange segments and spring onions in a bowl.

2 Make a dressing with the oil, lime juice, reserved orange juice and a seasoning of salt and pepper. Add to the salad and mix everything together. Chill for at least 30 minutes.

3 Toss once more to mingle the flavours thoroughly, then serve with the herbs sprinkled on top.

DESSERTS
AND DRINKS

Avocado Cream

Creme de Abacate

*Avocados provide almost instant, refreshing and easy desserts. This is one of the most popular
'sobremesas' in Brazil.* **Serves 6–8**

3 ripe avocados

125 g/4½ oz caster sugar

juice of 1 lime

6 tablespoons milk

pinch of salt

3 tablespoons port wine

1 Halve the avocados lengthways and remove the stones. Spoon out the flesh from the skins, roughly chop and put the pieces in a bowl. Sprinkle with the sugar and lime juice. Cover and chill for 15 minutes.

2 Place the avocado mixture in a blender or food processor with the milk and salt and blend until smooth. Pass through a sieve, pressing with the back of a spoon.

3 Stir in the port. Heap into appropriate glasses and chill in the fridge for at least 1 hour. Serve chilled.

Blancmange

Manjar

Manjar (which means no more than 'eating' in Brazilian Portuguese) is short for manjar blanco. It is a well-loved dessert in Brazil, its simple clean taste and texture providing contrast to the very many rich egg and coconut puddings. **Serves 4–6**

1 In a saucepan, heat the milk with the rice flour, sugar and salt, whisking to dissolve the sugar and incorporate the flour.

2 Before the mixture boils, remove the pan from the heat and set it in another larger pan half-filled with boiling water. On a low heat, keeping the water simmering, cook for 15 minutes, stirring to make sure the mixture doesn't stick.

3 Pour into a buttered glass serving bowl. Leave to cool before transferring to the fridge to chill. Serve very cold with fruit conserves (*cocadas*).

1.2 litres/2 pints milk

225 g/8 oz rice flour

225 g/8 oz caster sugar

tiny pinch of salt

To serve:

fruit conserves (*cocadas*)

Caramel Custard

Caramela

This is the most loved dessert in the Spanish- and Portuguese-speaking world, where it is otherwise known as flan. *Served chilled in small cups or soufflé dishes, it is found in every eating place, and sold off the street in outlets such as* leiterias *(milk shops). If you have a vanilla pod, heat it with the milk as you scald it, instead of using vanilla essence.*

Makes 8 individual custards or 1 large one serving 6–8

1 Preheat the oven to 170°C/325°F/gas 3. Meanwhile, butter individual moulds that are 5–7.5 cm/2–3 in across or one large mould.

2 In a non-stick saucepan heat half the sugar, stirring with a wooden spoon until it melts and turns a deep brown. It must not burn. Pour a little melted sugar into each mould and tilt so that it spreads across the bottom.

3 Scald the milk by bringing it just up to boiling point, then remove from the heat and allow to cool. Add the vanilla essence.

4 In a bowl beat the whole eggs and egg yolks with the remainder of the sugar until it has dissolved. Beat in the milk and salt.

5 Pour the mixture through a sieve into the moulds (or large mould). Set the moulds in a deep oven tray and add very hot water to the tray to come half-way up the sides of the moulds. Bake for about 20 minutes, then turn down the temperature to 130°C/250°F/gas 1 and bake for a further 40 minutes. The custards are done when no liquid comes out if you press them. Or insert a knife blade, which should come out clean.

6 Leave to cool, then chill well. Before serving, invert each custard on to a plate. The sticky caramel mixture will have melted to make a delicious topping for this creamy treat.

butter for greasing

175 g/6 oz sugar

750 ml/1¼ pints milk

1 teaspoon pure vanilla essence

2 whole free-range eggs

6 free-range egg yolks

tiny pinch of salt

97

Golden Milk Pudding

Ambrosia

A typically rich Brazilian dessert, this is often accompanied by home-made Coconut and Pumpkin Preserve (page 124). When cooked the pudding turns a golden colour and takes on a granular texture. **Serves 4–6**

1 litre/1¾ pints milk

600 g/1 lb 5 oz caster sugar

9 free-range egg yolks

1 Place the milk in a non-stick saucepan, or large non-stick frying pan, and bring to boiling point. Remove from the heat at once.

2 Add the sugar and stir to dissolve. Beat in the egg yolks one by one.

3 Using a heat diffuser, return the pan to a low heat and leave to cook for 1 hour, stirring from time to time, until the mixture turns a delicate amber colour and the texture becomes grainy.

4 Leave to cool before serving.

Cassava Cake

Bôlo de Aipim

Aipim *is one of two distinct kinds of cassava. The cassava used for making flour first has to be processed to remove toxins, whereas* aipim *is ready to eat as a starchy vegetable, often boiled in chunks like potato. Once boiled it may be sliced into lengths and fried, to serve as an accompaniment to main courses. In this recipe grated* aipim *is the basis of a cool-tasting fresh cake. You need a piece of* aipim *weighing nearly 2 kg / 4½ lb in order to get 1.5 kg / 3 lb 5 oz of flesh, after peeling, grating and squeezing out moisture.* **Serves 6–8**

1 Preheat the oven to 180°C/350°F/gas 4.

2 Peel the *aipim* and grate it (use the grater attachment on a food mixer for preference, working in batches). Take handfuls of grated *aipim* between your two hands and squeeze out as much surplus starch and water as you can. You should end up with about 1.5 kg/3 lb 5 oz of grated flesh.

3 Put the grated *aipim* in a bowl and add the sugar, grated coconut, butter, egg yolk and salt. Mix in as much coconut milk as is needed to make a creamy cake mixture.

4 Make the glaze by dissolving the sugar in the coconut milk.

5 Butter a 23 cm/9 in cake tin, or a loaf tin, and pour the cake mixture into it. Bake for 40 minutes, brushing at intervals with the sugar and coconut milk glaze. To test if the cake is cooked, insert a skewer into the centre; it should come out clean.

6 Remove from the oven and leave to cool for 10 minutes before easing the cake out of its tin and on to a wire rack.

2 kg/4½ lb *aipim*

225 g/8 oz caster sugar

55 g/2 oz freshly grated coconut

55 g/2 oz butter *melted*

1 free-range egg yolk

pinch of salt

375 ml/12 fl oz coconut milk (see page 13)

butter for greasing

For the glaze:

1 tablespoon caster sugar

2 tablespoons coconut milk

Doraçy Biscuits

Biscoitos de Doraçy

These are a feature of the Mato Grosso, the flat pampas lands in the middle of Brazil. The Mato is the equivalent of the bush in Australia. Although called biscuits, these are more like little cakes, plaited into a figure of eight with an extra twist, the ends linked to each other. They are fried golden brown, like a doughnut, and served with tea. **Makes 8**

1 free-range egg

1½ teaspoons caster sugar

20 g/¾ oz butter *softened*

225 g/8 oz plain white flour

1 packet easy-blend dried yeast

oil for deep-frying

1 In a bowl, beat the egg with the sugar until thick and creamy, then beat in the butter.

2 Sift the flour into a bowl, adding the yeast. Mix the flour and the egg and butter mixture together, kneading into a soft dough. You may need to add a teaspoon or two of water if too dry. Cut into 8 equal portions.

3 Shape each portion into a ball and roll out on a floured board into a thin sausage about 25 cm/10 in long. Take it by its two ends, cross it over to make a figure eight, and then make a second cross-over, pinching the end to seal. Cover with a cloth and leave to rise for 30 minutes.

4 Half fill a deep pan with cooking oil and heat until quite hot (about 170°C/330°F, not as hot as for chips). Deep fry the *biscoitos* four at a time, turning them over when brown on one side, to brown the other. Remove with a slotted spoon and drain on kitchen paper. Like doughnuts, these are best served hot.

Coconut Flan

Quindão

Coconut is the prime ingredient in literally dozens of Brazilian desserts for which the country is justly renowned. It was the Portuguese nuns who brought to Brazil the secrets of making egg-based desserts flavoured with almonds. The workers from the slave plantations who learnt these skills saw they could substitute coconut for almonds, and thus provide themselves with a living by selling the desserts on the streets. The quindão is a large tart; quindim are tiny ones, made by the same method. They are sold everywhere in Brazil today, especially in pastry shops as a tea-time treat. **Makes one 23 cm/9 in tart**

4 whole free-range eggs

4 free-range egg yolks

450 g/1 lb icing sugar

50 g/1¾ oz butter *softened* **plus extra for greasing**

100 g/3½ oz freshly grated coconut or desiccated coconut

caster sugar for dusting

1 Whisk the whole eggs and yolks until smooth. Beat in the icing sugar, then add the butter and finally the grated coconut.

2 Preheat the oven to 180°C/350°F/gas 4. Meanwhile, butter a non-stick flan tin, 23 cm/9 in in diameter, and dust it with a little caster sugar. Pour the custard mixture into the pan. Stand it in a roasting tin and pour enough hot water into the roasting tin to come just above half-way up the sides of the flan tin. Bake for 40 minutes, checking towards the end to see if it is done. The top should be dry, and a skewer pushed into the centre should indicate whether it has set. If necessary, bake for an extra 10–15 minutes.

3 Leave to cool completely before attempting to turn it out. Loosen the edges with a palette knife, then cover with an upturned plate and tip it out, upside down.

Note: smaller flans (*quindim*) can be made in little individual cake tins and set in a roasting tin to bake, as above. They will take about 20 minutes to cook.

Sweet Potato Tart

Torta de Batata Doce

Brazilians are very fond of the sweet potato. It is used widely in soups, served as a vegetable accompaniment to main courses and made into desserts. This very rich, treacly tart can also be made with pumpkin, the dense sort grown in the Americas (which can sometimes be bought as a purée in cans). **Serves 6–8**

1 Preheat the oven to 200°C/400°F/gas 6. Set the sweet potatoes in an oven dish and bake for about 1 hour, or until soft. When cool enough to handle, peel and mash with a fork to make a purée. (If using pumpkin, bake in the same way.)

2 For the pastry, put the flour, sugar, baking powder and butter in a food processor and process until the mixture resembles breadcrumbs. Add the egg yolks and cream, and process to a smooth dough. Roll into a ball, wrap with cling film and chill for 30 minutes.

3 Preheat the oven to 190°C/375°F/gas 5.

4 In a non-stick saucepan heat the sweet potato purée with the sugar and coconut milk, stirring until the sugar dissolves. Remove from the heat and add the drained sultanas, cinnamon and vanilla essence. Leave to cool.

5 Roll out the pastry on a floured board and use to line a 25 cm/10 in tart or flan dish. Stand on a baking tray. With a palette knife spread the sweet potato mixture evenly in the pastry case, then press in the chopped nuts. Bake for 25–30 minutes, or until the pastry is brown. Eat warm or cold.

1 kg/2¼ lb sweet potatoes

375 g/13 oz caster sugar

150 ml/5 fl oz coconut milk (see page 13)

150 g/5 oz sultanas *soaked in Madeira or sweet wine until plump*

2 teaspoons ground cinnamon

1 teaspoon pure vanilla essence

150 g/5 oz shelled peanuts, cashews, pecans, almonds or Brazil nuts *skinned and coarsely chopped*

For the pastry:

200 g/7 oz plain flour

125 g/4½ oz caster sugar

1 teaspoon baking powder

55 g/2 oz butter *cubed*

1 free-range egg yolk

75 ml/2½ fl oz double cream or crème fraîche

Heavenly Bacon

Toucinho de Céu

Rashers of ham or bacon describe the shape and colour of these rich little desserts served in a caramelized syrup. Heavenly is how they taste. **Makes 20 or more**

1 In a large bowl, using a whisk, beat the egg yolks to a ribbon consistency, that is until the mixture thickens and lightens in colour and comes away from the sides of the bowl in ribbons.

2 Butter a medium-sized pudding basin and pour in the egg mixture. Stand the basin in a saucepan of water heated to simmering point, but not boiling. Allow to cook until the mixture firms to a jelly-like consistency without hardening completely, about 15–20 minutes. Remove from the pan of water and leave to cool completely. Then turn the egg mixture out of the basin and cut into thin slices, like rashers of bacon.

3 In a non-stick pan, heat 2 tablespoons of the sugar, stirring until it melts and caramelizes, turning an appetizing dark brown (but not blackening, which means it is burning). Remove from the heat at once and place the base of the pan in a bowl of cold water to arrest the cooking.

4 Return the pan to the heat and add 1 litre / 1¾ pints water, stirring to dissolve the caramel. Add the remaining sugar and dissolve it, then cook to a thick sugar syrup. Add the lemon zest and cinnamon. Simmer the syrup for 10 minutes.

5 Add the 'rashers' of egg yolk and simmer gently for a further 10 minutes or until they are well soaked. With a slotted spoon remove them to a serving plate. Boil the remaining sugar syrup for 5–10 minutes to evaporate some of the moisture. Pour the thick syrup over the heavenly bacon and leave to cool. A sticky treat, served cold.

12 free-range egg yolks

butter for greasing

750 g/1 lb 10 oz sugar

grated zest of ½ lemon

½ cinnamon stick

Mango Sorbet

Sorvete de Manga

Mango, passion fruit (maracujá), *pineapple* (abacaxi) *and guava* (goiaba) *all make the most delicious sorbets. But these are only a few of the many sorbet flavours offered in Brazilian cafés and restaurants – many more sorbets are made with unusual tropical fruits that are not exported.* **Serves 4–6**

200 g/7 oz caster sugar

4 ripe mangoes (about 750 g/
1 lb 10 oz)

juice of 1 lime

1 Make a sugar syrup by dissolving the sugar in 125 ml/4 fl oz water and bringing to the boil, stirring. Allow to cool completely.

2 Peel the mangoes and cut away the flesh from their flat stones. Purée the flesh in a blender in batches, adding the lime juice.

3 Mix the purée into the sugar syrup. Freeze in an ice-cream maker if you have one, following the manufacturer's instructions. Or pour into a shallow ice tray and put into the freezer; every 30 minutes remove the tray and beat the mixture with a fork or whisk to break up ice crystals as they form, then return to the freezer. Repeat this three or four times until the sorbet sets.

4 Remove the sorbet from the freezer to the refrigerator 20 minutes before serving.

Mother-in-law's Eyes

Olhas de Sogra

Another evocatively named sweet, this consists of prunes stuffed with a coconut mixture, the filling representing the eyeball and pupil quite realistically. Olhas de sogra are often sold in sweet shops, where a bizarre, extremely realistic effect is achieved. It is possible to buy very good quality pitted prunes, but those from Agen in France have the best flavour. Serve with strong coffee (removing the clove before eating). **Makes about 30**

1 To make the filling, dissolve the sugar in 100 ml/3½ fl oz boiling water. Off the heat stir in the grated coconut. Beat in the egg yolks, one by one. Using a heat diffuser, return to the heat and stir until the mixture thickens. Remove and leave to cool.

2 Open up each prune to receive the stuffing, smoothing in a mixture of coconut filling to represent the eyeball. Artistically place a clove at the centre of each to make the pupil of the mother-in-law's eye.

3 Dredge each sweet in a bowl of icing sugar. Serve in paper sweet cases.

200 g/7 oz sugar

250 g/9 oz freshly grated coconut

2 free-range egg yolks

750 g/1 lb 10 oz large prunes
stones removed

whole cloves

icing sugar for dredging

Students' Cakes

Bolinho de Estudante

Tapioca, one of the by-products of processing cassava, is used in both savouries and puddings. These are easily made deep-fried cakes. **Makes about 12**

250 g/9 oz tapioca flour

55 g/2 oz caster sugar

55 g/2 oz freshly grated coconut

250 ml/9 fl oz milk

pinch of salt

flour for dusting

oil for deep-frying

ground cinnamon

icing sugar

1 In a bowl, mix together the tapioca flour, caster sugar, coconut, milk and salt, then add enough water (about 120–250 ml/4–9 fl oz) to make a smooth paste. Leave it to stand for 15 minutes.

2 Roll out on floured board to 1 cm/½ in thickness. Use a small cup or glass to cut out discs about 5 cm/2 in across.

3 Deep-fry in hot oil at 180°C/350°F until golden brown on both sides. Drain on kitchen paper, then sprinkle with cinnamon and icing sugar.

Angels' Cheeks

Papos de Anjo

Its name betrays its convent origins — this is one of many desserts deriving from the Portuguese nuns who first came to Brazil in the fifteenth century, bringing with them the skills in the making of egg and almond sweets learnt from the Moors. **Makes 12 medium-sized cakes**

2 free-range eggs *separated*

4 free-range egg yolks

15 g/½ oz plain flour

½ teaspoon baking powder

butter for greasing

For the sugar syrup:

250 g/9 oz sugar

½ teaspoon pure vanilla essence

1 Preheat the oven to 200°C/400°F/gas 6.

2 In a bowl whisk the 2 egg whites until firm, then beat in the 6 egg yolks one by one. Beat in the flour with the baking powder, and continue beating until the mixture thickens.

3 Lightly butter a tray of 12 straight-sided cake moulds, each about 6 cm/2½ in across. Pour the mixture into the moulds to fill each to two-thirds. Bake for 20 minutes, checking if the cakes are cooked by inserting a skewer into the centre; it should come out clean when you remove it. They will puff up and turn a lovely golden colour.

4 Dissolve the sugar in 250 ml/9 fl oz water, then bring to the boil. Remove from the heat. When cool, add the vanilla essence.

5 When the cakes are cool, remove them from the moulds, place them in a suitable shallow dish and pour the syrup over them, allowing it to soak in.

Dreams
Sonhos

These sweet desserts, made with polvinho *(tapioca flour), are typically Brazilian. They puff up when deep-fried, and are best eaten hot and crisp from the pan.* **Makes 12–16**

1 In a non-stick saucepan heat the milk with the granulated sugar and salt, stirring to dissolve. As it bubbles to the boil, tip in all the tapioca flour, stirring with a wooden spoon. Remove from the heat at once and beat until the mixture leaves the side of the pan, forming a hot ball of dough.

2 Beat in the egg yolks one at a time, mixing throroughly before adding the next.

3 Heat a pan of oil for deep-frying to about 180°C/350°F. Using a large teaspoon, shape balls of the dough and fry, a few at a time, until golden on all sides.

4 Drain on kitchen paper, then roll in a saucer of icing sugar mixed with cinnamon. Eat while hot.

250 ml/9 fl oz milk

1 tablespoon granulated sugar

¼ teaspoon salt

150 g/5 oz fine tapioca flour

4 free-range egg yolks

oil for deep-frying

2 tablespoons icing sugar

1 teaspoon ground cinnamon

Longings

Saudades

How much is expressed in this simple word — perhaps longings of Portuguese immigrants for family and homeland? This is one of the simplest forms of the many hundreds of sweets made with egg yolks and sugar, and is like a cross between a macaroon and a meringue.

Makes 20

5 free-range egg yolks

250 g/9 oz caster sugar

250 g/9 oz fine sago flour

1 Preheat the oven to its lowest setting.

2 In a mixing bowl whisk the egg yolks to the ribbon stage – until thick and light in colour, and leaving the side of the bowl in ribbons. Beat in the sugar.

3 Pour in the flour bit by bit, mixing into a paste with a wooden spoon until you can use your hands for mixing. Add enough flour so that you can shape the paste into balls half the size of an egg.

4 Lay the balls on a baking tray and put into the oven. Leave until well dried out, which can take several hours. The time needed depends on your oven.

Milk Sweet

Doce de Leite

This is a popular accompaniment to desserts, similar to clotted cream. It's sometimes eaten on bread or with cakes, and sometimes with a spoon just as it is. One common Latin-American version is made by immersing an unopened can of sweetened condensed milk in water and simmering for several hours, after which (taking care to let it cool thoroughly before opening) it will have turned to a soft toffee-like consistency. Doce de leite forms little lumps after prolonged cooking and so should be removed from the heat when it starts to brown. **Serves 6–8**

1 Put the milk and sugar in a saucepan and bring to a rapid boil, stirring with a wooden spoon until the sugar dissolves.

2 Add the vanilla pod and cinnamon. Turn down the heat to the lowest possible and simmer for about 1½ hours, stirring from time to time to prevent sticking.

3 As the water in the milk evaporates, the mixture thickens and reduces in volume. Eventually the dense sugars begin to brown and form lumps. Remove and discard the vanilla pod and cinnamon sticks. Take off the heat and leave to cool, then chill.

4 Serve chilled. *Doce de leite* will keep in the fridge for a week.

3 litres/4¼ pints milk

1 kg/2¼ lb sugar

1 vanilla pod

2 sticks cinnamon

Toffee Fudge Sweets

Brigadeiro

One of the universal children's party sweets in Brazil, this is a kind of milky toffee.
Makes about 40 pieces

1 In a non-stick saucepan, over a heat diffuser, gently heat the condensed milk with the butter, chocolate and milk. Stir with a wooden spoon until the mixture comes away from the sides of the pan.

2 Remove from the heat and add the vanilla essence.

3 On a cool buttered surface (a marble slab would be ideal) spread the mixture with a palette knife.

4 When cool enough to handle, cut the mixture into 40 pieces. With your hands, roll each into a small ball and then roll in chocolate vermicelli to coat all over.

5 If you have suitable small sweet moulds, press the toffee fudge in to shape the pieces. Lay them on a tray lined with greaseproof paper and allow to cool thoroughly and set.

2 x 450 g/15 oz cans condensed milk

20 g/¾ oz unsalted butter

3 tablespoons grated dark chocolate (with 70% cocoa solids)

100 ml/3½ fl oz milk

5 drops of pure vanilla essence

butter for greasing

chocolate vermicelli

Nut Brittle

Pé-de-Moleque

This is a street sweet sold in towns and cities alike, but it is easy enough to make at home. Use other nuts to taste, such as chopped castanha de Pará *(Brazil nuts), almonds or hazelnuts. This recipe uses the cheapest nuts —* amendoim, *or peanuts. Muscovado sugar gives a luscious, rich flavour, while white sugar lets the nuts speak for themselves.* Moleque *is a mischievous boy, urchin or beggar and his* pé *is his foot. So this is Ragamuffin's Foot.*

Makes about 1 kg/2¼ lb

500 g/1 lb 2 oz unsalted peanuts

1 kg/2¼ lb muscovado sugar or white granulated sugar

butter for greasing

1 Toast the peanuts under the grill or on a low heat in a very lightly oiled frying pan. Keep shaking the nuts so that they toast evenly. If you cook them too quickly they will burn on the outside, remaining raw inside.

2 Remove from the heat. When cool enough to handle, rub the nuts in a tea towel to loosen the flaky skins. Roughly chop the peanuts.

3 Bring 1 litre/1¾ pints water to the boil. Pour in the sugar, stirring until it dissolves. Boil rapidly and, when the syrup begins to thicken, add the peanuts. Continue boiling until the brittle is ready, stirring to prevent sticking. To test, remove a little with a wooden spoon and dip it into a bowl of cold water set beside the cooker; if the brittle hardens, it is ready. If you have a sugar thermometer, this should be the hard crack stage, 146°C/295°F.

4 While the brittle is boiling, half fill the sink with cold water. As soon as the brittle is ready, remove the pan from the heat and gently dip the base into the cold water for a few moments, to stop the cooking.

5 Pour the brittle on to two buttered flat tins, each about 30 x 20 cm/ 12 x 8 in. When almost cool, make cuts all over the surface to mark out roughly shaped pieces. When cold break the brittle along these lines.

Passion Fruit Cocktail

Batida de Maracujá

The batida *is the cousin of the* caipirinha, *a chilled white rum cocktail with freshly pressed fruit juice. The main difference between a lime* batida *and* caipirinha *is that the former is strained before serving.* Batidas *are made with every kind of fruit juice, from pineapple juice to coconut milk.* Maracujá *(passion fruit) is one of the most liked, evoking the heady scents of tropical Brazil.* **Makes 4 drinks**

1 Cut the passion fruits in half and scoop out the flesh into a sieve. Press with the back of a spoon to strain the juice from the seeds. (The seeds and skins can be heated through with a glass of water and 1 tablespoon of sugar, then strained and cooled, to make a tart sauce which you can add to a fruit salad or thicken with cornflour to serve as a sauce.)

2 Slip the ice cubes into a small plastic bag, place on a chopping board and reduce them to splinters using a rolling pin or similar.

3 Combine the *cachaça*, passion fruit juice, sugar and crushed ice, and shake well.

4 Serve in glasses you have chilled in the freezer.

8 wrinkled passion fruits

20 ice cubes

300 ml/½ pint *cachaça*

4 teaspoons caster sugar

White Rum Sour

Caipirinha

The most famous of traditional Brazilian cocktails, this is drunk before a meal to give you a kick-start. The ice is cooling, the freshness of the lime arouses the appetite and the concentration of alcohol animates conversation. Caipirinha actually translates as 'yokel' or 'country bumpkin', perhaps indicating the rough and ready way the limes are coarsely chopped into the drink. There are literally hundreds of brands of cachaça, *the national spirit, a white rum made from cane sugar, the best very good indeed. Modern twists are* caipirosca *with vodka instead of* cachaça, *and* caipirissima, *made with Bacardi rum.*

Makes 4 drinks

2 limes

16 ice cubes

4 teaspoons caster sugar

300 ml/½ pint *cachaça*

1 With a sharp knife cut the limes into quarters and remove the coarse central membranes. Slice the lime quarters into small, even chunks.

2 Put the ice cubes into a plastic bag, place on a chopping board and reduce them to splinters using a rolling pin or similar.

3 Combine the limes and sugar in mortar (skilful barmen do all this in individual glasses in front of you), pounding them together. Add the *cachaça* and crushed ice and shake well, preferably in a cocktail shaker or in a jug with the top covered. Don't use a blender – the pieces of lime must remain whole.

4 Serve in glasses you have chilled in the freezer.

Opposite *White Rum Sour and Passion Fruit Cocktail (page 119)*

Coconut Milk Shake

Refresco de Côco

A deceptively simple, cooling and nourishing drink for a hot day. This recipes uses skimmed milk, which is light and refreshing, although semi-skimmed or full fat milk is just as tasty if more filling. **Makes 4 drinks**

1 coconut

1 litre/1¾ pints skimmed milk

caster sugar to taste

1 Pierce two of the three holes at the base of the coconut and pour out the liquid (*água de côco*), reserving it. Strain the liquid in a sieve to remove fibres and dust which fall from the shell.

2 Break open the coconut using a hammer or other implement. Cut the shards of flesh from the shell. Cut the hard brown skin from the coconut flesh, then grate, using a food mixer with a grater attachment to spare your fingers.

3 Heat the milk, without boiling, and stir in the grated coconut. Remove from the heat and put aside to infuse for 40 minutes. Pour the coconut-flavoured milk through a cloth into a bowl, tightening the cloth to extract all the juice, like wringing out a T-shirt. Combine with the *água de côco*.

4 Add a little caster sugar to taste, stirring to dissolve, and add a little water to dilute the drink. Chill well. Serve from the fridge with ice cubes.

Limeade

Limonada Suissa

Limonada suissa is the name given in Brazil to the national drink of limeade, the pungent green limão *being the nearest citrus fruit they have to lemon.* **Makes 6–8 drinks**

1 Pare the zest from 1 lime. Put the zest in a saucepan with the sugar and 125 ml/4 fl oz water and bring to the boil, stirring until the sugar has dissolved. Remove from the heat and leave to cool completely. Remove the lime zest.

2 Squeeze the juice from the limes and add to the sugar syrup. Chill.

3 Serve from the fridge, adding crushed ice and water to dilute to taste.

8 limes

250g /9 oz caster sugar

Coconut and Pumpkin Preserve

Cocada com Abóbora

Brazil has many unconventional preserves not found in Europe, such as sugared beetroot, sweetened carrot and many based on pumpkin, a native vegetable. Unusually pumpkin is combined with coconut in this preserve. **Makes about 2 x 450 g/1 lb jars**

about 250 g/9 oz *abóbora*
(or use butternut or kabocha
squash) to give 150 g/5 oz flesh

500 g/1 lb 2 oz sugar

2 cloves

150 g/5 oz freshly grated coconut
or 125 g/4½ oz desiccated
coconut

1 Peel the *abóbora* and remove the fibres and seeds. Cut the flesh into small pieces.

2 Bring 1 litre/1¾ pints of water to the boil in a saucepan. Add the sugar and stir to dissolve.

3 Add the *abóbora* and the cloves. Quickly bring to the boil and cook until the *abóbora* breaks down into a purée, stirring to avoid sticking or burning. When it thickens, stir in the coconut and simmer for 10 more minutes to allow the coconut flavours to combine with the pumpkin.

Caramelized Coconut Preserve

Dissolve 600 g/1 lb 5 oz sugar in 250 ml/9 fl oz water. Off the heat stir in 150 g/5 oz freshly grated coconut or 125 g/4½ oz desiccated coconut, then simmer on a low heat for 10 minutes. Leave to cool.

White Coconut Preserve

Make the Caramelized Coconut Preserve using milk instead of water and flavouring it with 2–3 cloves.

Guava Paste
Goiabada

The acidic, highly scented guava, varying from raw green to pretty yellow and pink, is a very popular fruit in Brazil and is used in conserves, jellies, mousses and drinks. A thick jellied paste of guava is usually found on the breakfast table to be eaten with a slice of cheese, perhaps the squeaky, fresh white cheese of Minas Gerais. Goiabada is a cousin of the Spanish mermelada, or quince paste, which is also popular in Brazil.

Makes about 500 g/1 lb 2 oz

1 Cut off the skins of the guavas and scrape out the pips. Push the pulp through a fine sieve. You should be left with about 500 g/1 lb 2 oz puréed pulp. Weigh out an equal amount of sugar.

1 kg/2¼ lb ripe guavas
about 500 g/1 lb 2 oz sugar
butter for greasing

2 Put the sugar in a large pan and add 125 ml/4 fl oz water. Bring to the boil, stirring to dissolve the sugar, then boil to the soft ball stage (115°C/239°F on a sugar thermometer). You can test by dipping a teaspoon of the boiling sugar syrup into a bowl of cold water; if the syrup can be shaped into a small ball, it is ready.

3 Add the guava purée and stir with the sugar syrup until the mixture comes away from the sides of the pan. Remove from the heat. Spread on a buttered baking tray and leave to cool.

4 Once cold and set, cut into squares and wrap in greaseproof paper to store in airtight tins.

Page numbers in *italic* refer to the illustrations

I would like to thank the many Brazilian friends who have, over the years, shared with me their love of Brazil and introduced me to its vibrant culture: in particular Marcia Magnavita Marques da Silva and her family; Betty Chiaratti, Margaret van Peterkin, David and Zelia Edwards. Among others who have offered inspiration and information: chef Jean-Yves Poirey and Teresa Pedruzzi of Le Meridien, Copacabana, Rio de Janeiro, and chef Adauto Rodrigues of the São Paulo Hilton, and in London, Andrew and Alberina Hunton of Sabor do Brasil, Highgate. At the Brazilian Embassy in London, Tovar da S. Nunes and Maria Graça-Fish.

I owe a special debt to Elisabeth Lambert Ortiz, the food writer most influential in awakening us to the Latin-American culinary world in books such as *The Book of Latin-American Cooking* (Penguin) and *The Flavours of Latin America* (Latin-American Bureau, London). Among Brazilian books which convey the unique spirit of the North-east are *A Culinaria Baiana*, produced by the SENAC cookery school in Salvador de Bahia, and Darwin Brandão's *A Cozinha Baiana*.

I would also like to thank the Conran Octopus team for their warm support, managing editor Kate Bell, art director Leslie Harrington and copy editor Norma MacMillan, as well as Suzannah Gough and Jenni Muir, who first invited me to write this book.

And finally, thanks to my wife, Heather, and my children, Alex and Georgia, who share my passion for all things Brazilian.

PUBLISHER'S ACKNOWLEDGEMENTS

The publisher would like to thank the following photographers for their kind permission to reproduce the photographs in this book:

6–7 James Davis Travel Photography; 38–39 Anthony Blake Photo Library/Guy Moberly; 60–61 Travel Ink/Charlie Marsden; 84–85 Carlos Freire/Hutchison Library; 112–113 Sue Cunningham/SCP

Also thanks to Hilary Bird for the index, Susanna Tee for recipe testing and Sarah Widdecombe for proofreading.